THE AMERICAN WEST

The Invention of a Myth

Americans have chosen to invest one small part of their history, the settlement of the western wilderness, with extraordinary significance. The lost frontier of the 1800s remains not merely a source of excitement and romance but of inspiration, because it is seen as providing a set of unique and imperishable core-values; individualism, self-reliance and a pristine sense of right and wrong. As a construct of the imagination, America's creation of the West is unique. Since this construct has little to do with history, *The American West* argues that our beliefs about the West amount to a modern functional myth.

In addition to presenting a sustained analysis of how and why the myth originated, David Murdoch demonstrates that the myth was invented, for the most part deliberately, and then outgrew the purposes of its inventors.

The American West answers questions which have too often been either begged or ignored. Why should the West become the focus for myth in the first place, and why, given the long process of western settlement, is the cattleman's West so central and the cowboy, of all prototypes, the mythic hero? And why should the myth have retained its potency up to the last decade of the twentieth century?

David Hamilton Murdoch is Principal Teaching Fellow in the School of History at the University of Leeds. Educated at Sidney Sussex College, Cambridge, and Liverpool University, David Hamilton Murdoch has written widely on American History and has been a Fellow of the Royal Historical Society since 1980.

THE AMERICAN WEST

The Invention of a Myth

David H. Murdoch

Welsh Academic Press

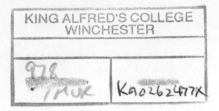
First published in Wales by Welsh Academic Press 2001

Welsh Academic Press is an imprint of
Ashley Drake Publishing Ltd
PO Box 733
Cardiff
CF14 2YX
www.ashleydrake.com
post@ashleydrake.com

ISBN
186057 0119 (hardback)
186057 0127 (paperback)

© David Hamilton Murdoch 2001

A CIP catalogue record for this book is available from
the British Library.

Typeset by WestKey Limited, Falmouth, Cornwall

CONTENTS

ACKNOWLEDGEMENTS

My first thanks probably should go to Bill Boyd, who introduced me to the magic formula, and to John Wayne, who committed me to a lifetime's interest in the mythical West. More recently, I am grateful to Christopher Andrew for persuading me to begin this book; to the staff of the Brotherton Library for their patience and good humour in dealing with my endless inter-library loan requests; and to Bill Speck for his constant support and encouragement.

D.H.M.
University of Leeds,
July 2000

PREFACE

No other nation has taken a time and place from its past and produced a construct of the imagination equal to America's creation of the West. And having created it, America promptly and success - fully exported it, so that it became the property of much of the world, which is my excuse as an outsider for having the temerity to write about it. Like most people of my generation, I came to the West through the movies. In Britain of the late 1940s and 1950s we knew there was a world better than the one we were obliged to inhabit, and Hollywood kept giving us glimpses of it. I enjoyed just about every kind of American film; but the Western captivated me. Indeed, I found that its images and stereotypes, its carefully observed rituals and its implicit world-view were mesmeric. It was very much later that I began to ask why. Meanwhile, it is comforting to note that I was in good company, for Westerns have been Hollywood's most popular single genre; outdistancing thrillers, comedies, dramas and musicals, they account for a quarter of total output.

I came to the West again and from a new direction when trying to understand how Americans think about themselves. This of course was serious academic enquiry and not meant to involve my passion for Westerns, which I had managed to keep a secret vice. Following a well-trodden path in trying to perceive relationships between poli - tics, culture and ideas, I was obliged to contend with the obvious: for most of this century, Americans have assigned the West a remarkable role. As an episode in the history of the United States, the conquest of the West is deemed to have special – indeed, crucial – significance. For long it has been seen as a national epic and it was held to have enshrined an experience whose effects, they have chosen to believe, made Americans different from other peoples. Specifically, that ex - perience seemed to be regarded as defining uniquely American char - acteristics and values – traditionally, individualism, self-reliance and an instinctive commitment to democracy.

This is not a truth which is self-evident. If these qualities define Americanism, it is not easy to see why the process of settling the West is their most obvious determinant. After all, who participated? In 1900 ten million people lived west of the Mississippi; sixty-six million lived east of it. As far as the frontier experience is concerned, a decade after the frontier was supposed to have closed, spectators outnumbered players by nearly seven to one. The thirty-five years following the Civil War had seen the most dramatic phase of the great westward migra - tion, but those same years saw the nature of America changed funda - mentally and permanently. The nation increased its population two-and-a-half times, absorbed over eleven million immigrants, saw much of that growth concentrated in mushrooming cities, became a huge industrial power generating enormous wealth and translated that strength into a major role in international affairs. These things, and the interaction between them, transformed not only America but Americans. It can be persuasively argued that, in terms of ways of thinking and behaving, these factors had changed the eighty-seven per cent of the population of 1900 who did not live in the West a good deal more decisively than the frontier experience. If this is so, then it can also be argued that these factors encouraged not individualism but conformity, not self-reliance but interdependence and a political system designed, as in other modern states, to blunt the thrust of grass-roots democracy.

Yet the 'frontier heritage' has the status of an axiom of nationality. Of course, Frederick Jackson Turner, who a century ago first gave the frontier effect the dubious accolade of academic respectability, and the historians who followed him, argued that the conquest of the West did not begin when settlers crossed the Mississippi. It began when seventeenth-century colonists first pushed inland from the coast and it took off in earnest when pioneers spilled over the Appalachian Mountains at the end of the eighteenth century, spreading over the next four decades through untamed country north to the Great Lakes and south to the Gulf of Mexico. The frontier, at any given point in time, was simply the farthermost edge of settlement. In this sense the process had been going on for two centuries before the pioneers pushed out on to the plains and it affected generation after generation as the nation grew, so that its effects became indelible, whatever other experiences might ensue.

But this advancing frontier is not the West of imagination and inspiration. The picture which most of us hold in our mind's eye is not the forests of Kentucky and Tennessee but the Great Plains and the mountains and deserts of the *real* West. Nor is the typical West - erner Daniel Boone protecting farmers from the Shawnee, or Davy

Crockett chasing bears; the real West is filled with cowboys driving cattle, lawmen confronting badmen, the cavalry hunting Apache and Sioux and wagon trains bringing civilisation with relentless inevita - bility. Our images derive from the screen and Hollywood proves the point: ten films all told have Daniel Boone as the central character, Crockett appears in eleven, Buffalo Bill Cody features in 47, Billy the Kid in 44, Wild Bill Hickok and Jesse James in 35 each, General Custer in 34 and Wyatt Earp in twenty-one. The West that excites admiration is also the Wild West.

When investigating the West as an idea, beyond a certain point Hollywood's images cannot be ignored. What the movies celebrate is not the two-and-a-half century-long conquest of the wilderness but its last thirty years, usually choosing as the arena the cattle kingdom. This raises some questions whose answers are too often taken for granted. Why has Hollywood concentrated on those particular thirty years, why that specific arena? Objectively, it is hard to see why they are intrinsically more exciting than, say, the forests of James Feni - more Cooper's Leatherstocking Tales, or the real and extraordinary feats of the Rocky Mountain trappers – both of which, in the nineteenth century, had their heyday as highly popular entertain - ment. But Westerns cannot be dismissed as merely another fashion in entertainment, precisely because they have eclipsed all rival visions of the frontier and their images have dominated our thinking about the West for the whole of this century.

Naturally, Hollywood is not history and nobody believes the West was like a Western. But if Westerns are fantasy, why so consistent a fantasy? Ignorant critics are prone to remark that all Westerns are the same. In fact, plot variation has been enormous over the last ninety years; but it is also true that, more than any other genre, the Western operates within conventions and these conventions are not the framework but the genre's essence. Westerns are about conflict: they consistently pit the lone hero, often as not on behalf of the community, against enemies who impede 'progress' – the land itself, Indians, criminals and those who would abuse power. In other words they affirm the values of individualism, self-reliance and the demo - cratic impulse.

Hollywood's conventions thus interlock with the heroic and epic story which has been the popular version of the history of the West. A whole generation of historians has been chipping away at that version and recently they have embarked on structural demolition. As a result, precious little is left of the great epic and most of the heroes have turned out severe disappointments. Yet the impact of academic iconoclasm has been marginal. The 1980s saw President

Reagan confidently and persistently call for a revival of what he believed to be the pioneer spirit and frontier values. In the summer of 1991 the National Museum of American Art mounted an exhibition entitled 'The West as America: Reinterpreting Images of the Fron-tier.' The reinterpretation sought to reveal those images as carefully contrived propaganda on behalf of an aggressive, imperialistic and racist white society. The exhibition promptly caused a political furore. Politicians (many of them before they saw it) greeted it with outrage and threats to the Museum's funding, while the press rose in wrath; in the words of the *Wall Street Journal*, the exhibition was 'an entirely hostile ideological assault on the nation's founding and history.'

It is difficult to imagine any other period of America's past exciting similar reactions. Presidents do not call on the spirit of Revolutionary patriots nor has academic historical revisionism in any period tradi-tionally attracted much more than a flicker of public interest. Even the recent assault of multiculturalism on the teaching of history in America's schools has yet to produce a serious political backlash in Washington. The reason is simple: the vision of the frontier heritage recently so staunchly defended by politicians and press and the images so consistently presented by the Western movie are not history, not even romanticised history: they are myth and the power of myth is not to be gainsaid.

Once introduce the word myth in connection with the West and there is an immediate tendency to brandish it about like a talisman to ward off rational discussion. Most of those who happily refer to the 'myth of the West' acknowledge its power while carefully avoiding answering the questions instantly raised – like, why should a modern nation have a myth at all, what purpose does it serve, and why should it be given widespread credence by an educated and sophisticated society? Those of us who take seriously the mythical West, and its expression in movies, were much indebted to Will Wright when, in 1975, he produced his challenging study *Six Guns and Society*. Wright offered a structural analysis of Western films as the American na-tional genre, arguing that the Western projected a myth of contempo-rary American society. Drawing on a range of disciplines, Wright took as his starting point the concept that myths, among other functions, mediate the conflicts and contradictions which societies generate and which cause deep-seated anxieties for their members. His analysis of Westerns thus aimed to reveal links between the structure of the myth, as revealed in films, and the conflicts emerging from the changing structure of American institutions.

As far as it goes, this was an interesting and provocative idea. Critics were quick to quarrel with the patterns and categories which

Wright imposed upon his selection of Westerns (the just criticism was that he had viewed too few). His central argument however remains illuminating and his conclusions perceptive:

> While other societies reaffirm themselves through religious
> rituals and traditional observances, we seem to accomplish
> this, at least in part, through a return to faith in the land
> of the West. In fact, it seems this land has become our
> tradition – a tradition based not on the West itself but on
> the myth of the West.

An historian however is left with some nagging questions. Wright does not suggest that the myth of the West was actually created by films, say, by Edwin Porter when he made *The Great Train Robbery* in 1903, or by the Essanay Company's marketing of the first cowboy star, Bronco Billy Anderson five years later, or by Bronco Billy's successors, William S. Hart and Tom Mix, or by directors like D.W. Griffith and Thomas Ince – let alone by John Ford or John Wayne. But if the film industry merely cashed in on the myth, and films became its most effective vehicle, then where did the myth come from? If myth is a response to disturbing tensions in a society, why did the United States pick on the West as a source? In all the long process of conquering the wilderness, why is the cattleman's West so central and why is the cowboy, of all prototypes, the hero? And what had the inhabitants of the West of reality to say about the West of myth?

In the following pages I attempt to answer these questions. Better scholars than I have reconstructed the past to reveal a West very different from that of myth. I have sought to explain why people thought about the West in the way they did, often in defiance of evidence and sometimes of common sense. It is clearly very difficult to determine what, at any given time, large numbers of people are thinking, and why. It is therefore necessary, for the purposes of my argument, to make some assumptions. Chief of these is that if consumers in a free-market economy persist in buying a product decade after decade, then the product has intrinsic appeal.

For the myth of the West was indeed a product and should be investigated as such. Generally speaking, with myths it cannot be taken for granted that one should begin at the beginning. Certainly, the experts are inclined to accept that the origins of the classical myths, or those of tribal societies, are beyond discovery. The myth of the West however has not been around from time out of mind, it is a reasonably accessible phenomenon; there is no need to assume that, like Topsy, it just growed. On the contrary, it is contended here that the origins of the myth can be clearly defined, indeed, can be dated with some precision. The Western myth was not some organic growth, mysteriously arising from the depths of the collective American unconscious (though indeed it ended there). It was deliberately invented by a relatively small number of mostly identifiable people with specific purposes in mind. It was they who focussed attention on the last phase of the conquest of the wilderness and they who made the cowboy a mythic hero. Their invention was then marketed with all the resources available in a market-oriented society. It succeeded beyond the inventors' hopes, for they struck a chord which immediately reverberated in the national psyche and which has continued to resonate down the years.

Chapter One

History through the Looking Glass

If we understand this part of our history, we will better understand how our people see themselves and the hopes they have for America.

Ronald Reagan, 1983

In March 1983 President Ronald Reagan took time off from affairs of state to open an exhibition, organised by the Library of Congress, entitled 'The American Cowboy.' His decision caused no surprise, not just because the press now and again liked to remind Americans of his brief career as a Western film star. Reagan himself had made very clear that he believed Americans should return to those older values which traditionally had been associated with America's pioneer heritage, values which somehow came especially out of the West. He was never to express it more clearly than in his address at the exhibition:

> If we understand this part of our history, we will better understand how our people see themselves and the hopes they have for America. Tales of Wild West men and women, from Kit Carson to Wild Bill Hickok, to Calamity Jane to Annie Oakley, are woven into the dreams of our youth and the standards we aim to live by in our adult lives. Ideals of courageous and self-reliant heroes, both men and women, are the stuff of Western lore...Integrity, morality and democratic values are the resounding themes.

Mr. Reagan did not of course, strictly speaking, understand this part of America's history. If he had, he would hardly have chosen such a pantheon. James Butler Hickok was a cold-blooded killer who spent most of his time gambling and chasing prostitutes. Martha 'Calamity Jane' Canary was a sad transvestite alcoholic, an inveterate liar who was reduced to exhibiting herself as a sideshow freak. Phoebe Anne Oakley Mozee was entirely the creation of showbusiness; the tiny trick-shot star was born in Ohio and had never been in the West when she joined Buffalo Bill Cody's Wild West show. In that gallery, Kit Carson stands alone as a remarkable figure. But no more remarkable than many of his contemporaries: Carson's public fame does not derive from his real-life exploits as a trapper and scout. Just like Hickok his heroic status was created by flamboyant journalism, reverent biographies and dime novels – the first two as much fiction as the last.

Yet in another sense Reagan understood American history very well indeed, for tales of the Wild West are part of Americans' folk-memory. Reagan knew that for three generations Americans had chosen to invest one particular episode in their past with an extraordinary significance, had turned the nineteenth-century frontier into the source of special American virtues and made its inhabitants into figures of legend. Reagan was simply demonstrating that he was one of those who, as British writer Jenni Calder has put it, 'believe in the legendary West not as historical fact but as historical force.' Reagan knew his words would strike a deep and resonating chord in the collective unconscious of America, would evoke an immediate, emotional and approving response. He was invoking the myth of the West.

Americans have come to regard the conquest of the Western wilderness as defining, in some special way, their characteristics as a unique people. Taken as a whole, that belief might be summarised as follows:

America possessed a unique resource which ensured a unique destiny; she faced to the West an empty continent. This vast area of free land offered the opportunity of independence to whoever could seize and use it, Easterner and European immigrant alike. The land was a wilderness; it was savage and cruel, like its aboriginal inhabitants the Indians – but it was potentially bountiful. In this land of terrible grandeur, nature was not so much an enemy as simply untamed: like the wild horses of its plains, it had to be broken to use. First the trails had to be blazed, Indians forced into retreat, the land opened. This was the work of the frontiersmen. But behind the frontiersmen came the pioneers, the farmers who took the free land, fought the wilderness and brought civilisation. In successive waves of an advancing tide, this process swept inexorably across the continent.

This immense challenge was met not by society as a whole, nor by corporate enterprise, nor least of all by government: the West was won by individuals. Imbued with a hardiness of spirit, pioneers were forced to rely upon themselves. To be sure, the pressures of frontier life imposed the need for co-operation within the community, but to a degree of the individual's choosing and within a milieu of equality. And as frontier communities arose, pioneers expressed their egalitarianism in creating basic democratic forms of government. Thus democracy was reborn again and again on the frontier and as the settlement advanced the democratic ideal suffused throughout America and became indelibly printed on the national consciousness.

The winning of the West was a time when issues were clear, when the endless and often shoddy compromises imposed by civilised society were temporarily in abeyance. Right and wrong, good and evil, were reduced to elemental simplicities. Problems without precedent required immediate solutions and, so that civilisation might replace savagery, those solutions sometimes involved an unprecedented level of violence. The extinction of the Indian menace, control of lawbreakers, the imposition of order within which freedom and independence could flourish – these things were achieved by force. The time of clear-cut issues was also the hour of the gun.

The frontier therefore brought forth men of extraordinary stature, men possessed of courage and skills to meet and overcome the dangers, so that the West could be made ready for the advance of civilisation. Thus the archetypal American hero is the frontier-tamer. Even those who put themselves beyond the law might become folk heroes, for if authority was arbitrary law might serve interest, not justice, and the outlaw appear just another rugged individualist.

In the last decade of the nineteenth century the conquest of the wilderness was completed and the frontier declared closed. Thus ended a crucial era in American history. The effects on all America could not however be erased. The frontier experience permanently shaped the American character: hardy, optimistic, egalitarian, impatient of intrusive authority. Above all, it defined America's core values: individualism, self-reliance, democratic integrity. For the future, the West had created a transformational process. In retrospect, the West was inspiring, dramatic, romantic – and wild.

This, give or take some elements, can be considered the received wisdom on the significance of the West. It had many sources: it drew on a variety of widely-held notions, not necessarily connected, which had started to coalesce in the 1890s, it was fed by writers and artists, supported by Westerners themselves and it was extended, developed and transmogrified by the media. Its early respectability owes a good deal to the work of the historian Frederick Jackson Turner. Whatever else it may be, it is not history. That is to say, as an interpretation of America's past it tells us less about the nineteenth-century West than it does about how twentieth-century American's have chosen to think about themselves. Reality, in so far as historians can reconstruct the past at all, was otherwise.

Was America's experience in meeting an empty continent and conquering a wilderness unique? Only in the sense that no two concatinations of circumstances can be identical, for comparisons can be made. The Victorian British, who were fascinated by the West and visited it in droves, were unimpressed with American claims of special qualities, the democratic impulse and heroic supermen. After all, British colonists had settled Canada, Australia, New Zealand and parts of Africa without too much fuss. Tsarist Russia's conquest of Central Asia and the settlement of Siberia was carried out at the behest of an autocracy and by military force but it was nevertheless a remarkable achievement.

Individualism may have existed in the West, but it did not flourish. The post-Civil War trans-Mississippi West was, according to the received wisdom, the arena for individual enterprise – in, for example, mining and cattle-ranching. The hardy lone prospector and placer miner rarely had any long-term success. Of the 100,000 hopefuls who poured out in the Pike's Peak rush of 1859, 50,000 never reached their goal and half of the remainder returned home immediately. Those who discovered a fortune usually failed to keep it: Henry Comstock sold his part-claim in the Nevada lode named after him for $11,000 in 1859; it ultimately produced $3 million. But the producers were usually not lucky or more determined individuals. Men like John Mackay and James Fair, two of the bonanza kings of the Comstock, were among those who represented mining as big business. Pursuing veins into deep mines and extracting precious metal from complex ores required technology and capital and these were available only to corporate enterprise. Effective exploitation meant industrialised mining and that demanded a disciplined labourforce, so that the typical Western miner by the mid-1870s was not a grizzled prospector with a shovel and a mule but a wage-labourer earning $3 a day.

Cattle-ranching followed a similar pattern. Raising cattle on the open range appeared to offer the perfect opportunity to combine the Western promise with the Puritan ethic: minimal overheads and eager markets (offering profits of over 30% on investment) should have guaranteed success for small men who believed in hard work and thrift. Examples can be found: John Iliff was a failed Pike's Peak miner who quit early, arrived broke in Wyoming in 1862 and in ten years built up a herd of 40,000 head. Just like mining, the beef bonanza however was dominated by corporate enterprise. Eastern corporations (and thus absentee owners) rapidly established an oligopoly and ruthlessly exploited the advantages of size and wealth. Some of the largest and most successful of the cattle enterprises were not American at all. The Prairie Cattle Company, which controlled 5 million acres of range in Texas, Colorado and New Mexico, was Scots. So were the XIT, Matador and Espuela [Spur] ranches in Texas, with ranges of 3 million, 1.5 million and half-a-million acres respectively. In Wyoming and Colorado the phrase 'cattle baron' was not a metaphor: the sons of the English aristocracy managed ranches for London-based companies whose boards of directors were filled with the peerage. Small wonder that the British were unimpressed with claims of a unique American achievement in the West.

The giant cattle companies, American or British, sought to maximise profits by efficiency and cost-cutting. The former often involved controlling water rights and safeguarding pasture; contrary to popular belief, ranchers were more likely to fence off range than farmers. Cost-cutting meant, among other things, keeping wages low for a dependent labour force. Thus the cowboy, central protagonist of the romantic drama of the West, was an itinerant wage-labourer, overworked and badly paid, without home, security or prospects. Few ever managed the great leap from drover to cattleman and the opportunity diminished further with the catastrophic collapse of the cattle boom in the late 1880s. Thereafter success depended even more heavily on access to capital and the application of sound business methods.

Most of those who achieved success in the West were, like as not, astute businessmen who diversified their interests with an eye for every opportunity. So far from resenting the presence of government, they sought to exploit it and often depended on it. Territorial, state and Federal government offices were useful prizes, while contracts to supply Indian reservations and the army were seen as a resource like the land itself. The notorious Santa Fe Ring, a combine of politicians, lawyers, traders and cattlemen which sought to monopolise business in New Mexico in the 1870s, was merely the most prominent example of a commonplace arrangement which made good business sense.

The role of corporate enterprise in the West stands uneasily with the proclaimed virtue of self-reliant individualism. It also belied the image of a phoenix-like democracy. Politics were quickly controlled by wealth and the power wealth brought. Montana by the end of the century was effectively in the hands of the Amalgamated Copper Company, which directly or indirectly employed over half the men in the state. Such power could be used with arrogant indifference to law: in 1892 the Wyoming Stock Growers' Association hired a private army of gunfighters to end the rustling threat they believed to be posed to their interests by the small ranchers and farmers of Johnson County. When the outraged locals rounded up the invaders, the cattlemen successfully appealed to Washington for the army to rescue them. Well might it be called the cattle kingdom, for it was not a republic.

Nowhere was the image so far from an often brutal reality than in the farmers' West. The great march of sturdy pioneers certainly took place, but not with the results that the received wisdom accorded it. The 1862 Homestead Act, for long regarded as the magic key to farmers' settlement of the Great Plains, offered a quarter section of 160 acres free, on condition that it was settled and worked for five years. The Act did not throw open the West to agriculture. It offered 84 million acres, but this was a fraction of the total available, for much of the best land had already been granted away: 213 million acres to railroads, 140 million to the states, 175 million reserved to Indians. Never was the Homestead Act the principal means of settling Western land: in the 1870s 300,000 homesteads were registered but 1.3 million new farms emerged on land which had been acquired from other sources. Speculators exploited loopholes to acquire the best sites and chicanery abounded. Semi-honest farmers might deviously acquire several quarter sections in order to use the extra as collateral for bank loans to raise capital. The image of the restless pioneer, forever moving on (so happily described in the *Little House* books of Laura Ingalls Wilder) could disguise an uglier practice. Contemporaries knew many 'chronic settlers' who filed for a quarter section, promptly raised a bank loan on its assumed value and equally promptly pocketed the money, abandoned the land to the bank and filed again under an assumed name elsewhere, to repeat the process over and over.

Long-term, farmers did not conquer the wilderness of the trans-Mississippi West; at best they wrested brief periods of prosperity from it, at worst they were conquered by it. The key to farming west of the 100th. meridian was water. There average rainfall dropped to 20 inches per year or less, and to 12 inches beyond a line roughly following the Kansas-Colorado and Nebraska-Wyoming borders. Farmers fooled themselves into believing they would find the 30 inch rainfall and lush lands of the Mid West on the Plains and they were encouraged by promoters – railroads, speculators and even government. For a decade between the mid-1870s and the mid-1880s nature fooled them too, for a freak period of heavy rain occurred. In 1887 a severe drought heralded the return of aridity; in 1894 only 8 inches of rain fell on a large part of the Western grasslands and the 1890s saw an agricultural catastrophe, as a result of which possibly as many as 200,000 settlers abandoned the West.

The answer appeared to be irrigation – but the costs were soon proved to be immeasurably beyond private resources. Pressure then built up to push the Federal government into a rescue operation and the result was the Reclamation Act of 1902. The costs of federally-sponsored irrigation projects were meant to be recouped by government land sales and charges to farmers, but the costs had, inevitably, been vastly underestimated and by 1923 less than 12% had been recovered. The Reclamation Act was a government support and bale-out operation; it made a mockery of claims of self-reliance and can be regarded, as some have termed it, the beginnings of the welfare state in the United States. The gadarene stampede of pioneer settlers into the West did not produce a prosperous agrarian democracy. Indeed, economists' analyses suggest many would have done better if they had stayed in the Mid West and East.

By the 1890s, those who controlled water rights dominated the Western economy and its society in the same way that business moguls did in the East. Speculation, fraud and a keen eye for taking advantage ensured that by the turn of the century over 80% of land beyond the Mississippi was owned by non-farmers. All in all, pioneers in the West had entered a very high-risk game: in addition to extremes of heat and cold, the devastating effects of hail, insect plagues and drought, they were at the mercy of market forces and ill-equipped to ride the roller-coaster of fluctuating costs and profits. By the last decade of the century success already belonged to agribusiness; like mining and ranching, the future lay, not with the hardy individual, but with large-scale, industrialised enterprise.

Legends may have made heroes of frontier-tamers but the raw material for these images needed a good deal of reshaping. The motley collection of adventurers, entrepreneurs and ruffians who comprised the elements of the leading edge of the advance into the West – hunters, trappers, scouts – were simply men who for one reason or another had chosen high-risk occupations. This should not diminish appreciation of their courage but few of them would have seen their lives as romantic until they were persuaded of it by what they read about themselves. The same is even more true of the cowboy, whose hard and precarious livelihood as a rural wage-labourer should have offered little in the way of material for the creation of the last and most influential of the actors in the pageant of the West. As for lawmen, once settlement had begun, most of the

West was rarely so disorderly that law officers had to present heroism as a job-qualification. On the contrary, the job, no more and no less onerous than today in small communities, was usually competed for and formed part of the local political patronage system. In potential trouble spots like the cattle railhead towns, citizens moved quickly to establish a proper police force – Dodge City had a uniformed force by 1881. As for outlaws, with the exceptions of the James brothers and perhaps the Doolin-Dalton gang, where special circumstances prevailed, all were detested and hounded by the communities on which they preyed.

Just how violent the West was has been a matter of considerable debate among historians. It has become fashionable to argue that it was not particularly violent at all – killings in the Kansas cowtowns averaged less than two per season in their heyday. Recent work has suggested that a good deal rests on how the statistics are presented; figures for mining townships in the Sierras in the 1860s and 1870s indicate a murder rate, on the basis of deaths per thousand of population, comparable with that of New York or Detroit in the 1980s. Rampant outbreaks of criminality were occasionally met with vigilantism – a vigilance committee controlled Virginia City, Montana Territory, between 1863 and 1865 and popularised the term 'vigilante.'* One analysis counts 210 vigilante movements in the West between 1849 and 1902. But vigilantism was not an invention of the Wild West: it had its roots in colonial times and followed settlement across the Appalachians into the South and the Mid West from the 1790s to the 1850s.

The present state of historical debate suggests that at certain times and in certain places, the West was indeed pretty violent. But this did not make it extraordinary: taken as a whole, the United States seems to have been in general a rather violent society in the nineteenth century, particularly so after the Civil War. Vivid, if not statistical, evidence is found in any issue of *Police Gazette*, a popular and sensational New York weekly which lovingly reported every crime it could find, North, South, East and West. Judging from its lurid pages, copiously illustrated, Americans of every kind and class, from street thugs to politicians, bludgeoned, stabbed and shot each other at the drop of a hat. Of course, it has been argued that such widespread violence percolated *back* from the frontier and eventually became a dubious aspect of the 'frontier heritage.' A different reading of the evidence suggests violence in the Eastern cities was one of the results of the instability created by mass immigration, coinciding

---

* Despite the publicity given to the San Francisco Vigilante Committee of 1856, the term does not appear to enter widespread use until the late 1860s.

with rapid native population growth, urbanisation and industrialisation.

Whatever else the West was, it was not a land of simple choices and clear-cut decisions; its pressures and problems may have been different from those in the East (in many cases they were indeed similar) but they were just as complex. Moreover, the vision of the received wisdom obscures or ignores what does not lie within its focus. For a start, that vision is white and in essence Anglo-Saxon. It pays no attention and gives no credit to the Spanish-American contribution to the winning of the West. When in 1848 two-fifths of Mexico was lost to the United States by war, the new Mexican-Americans of the Southwest and California were settlers whose experience rested on another and older conquest of the wilderness. The role of blacks was unrecognised until the belated 'discovery' of black cowboys in the 1960s; the tragic fate of the blacks who emigrated to Kansas in the 1870s, and the record of those Western states which passed legislation aimed at preventing black settlers in the 1850s and denying them voting rights in the 1870s, form no part of the saga of the West.

The Indian of course does. But by the time he had stopped oscillating between the roles of noble savage and fiendish redskin which public opinion had assigned him, he had become dehumanised. Much of the story presents the Indian as alien, implacable and irredeemable, an aspect (perhaps the most fearsome aspect) of the untamed land to be conquered by the march of progress. Though Westerners often seemed to imply it was their preferred solution, genocide however was not an option adopted at any point by the government of the United States. When, as the authorised version of the winning of the West evolved, it reversed its position and solemnly regretted the treatment of the Indians, it ignored the long-term implications of the historical evidence. The dismal record of broken treaties obscures the fact that treaties were consistently the preferred method of regulating Indian-white relations. That is to say, those relations rested on law and ultimately, as the last twenty-five years have shown, Indians could invoke their treaty rights (over fishing, land and water) finally to advantage. If it is responded that this is small comfort and that the law offered little hope of justice to Indians a century ago, neither did it to Eastern workers seeking industrial injury compensation, labour union activists – or small ranchers fighting the high-handed illegalities of the Wyoming Stock Growers' Association.

Despite its long acceptance as a statement of fact, a great phase of history did not come to an end because the Superintendant of the

Census mentioned, in passing, in his 1890 report that there was no longer a moving line of frontier settlement. History rarely offers examples of such startling discontinuity. New mining booms, the opening of the oil fields, the boost to farming by the Reclamation Act, each offered fresh opportunity in the West, while the problems too persisted into the twentieth century. The profound *influence* the conquest of the wilderness was deemed to have on American history derived from the emphasis placed on viewing it as an era with clearly defined limits. The origin of that emphasis, the insistence on a symbolic moment for the 'end of the West,' lies in the actual emergence, in codified form, of the cluster of images and ideas which accorded such primal significance to the frontier experience.

Those images and ideas about the West, its heroes and its meaning are, in terms of impact, America's greatest contribution to twentieth-century culture. And they are a genuine cultural artifact. They are not the distilled wisdom of the historical experience of the United States: they were invented to serve a specific purpose at a particular time. They were produced in response to the doubts and fears of America in the two decades on either side of the turn of this century. What is remarkable is the way they have transcended the reasons for their manufacture to impose an extraordinary and pervasive grip upon the imagination of succeeding generations.

Reagan was merely the latest, not the first, president to draw on the Western 'heritage' - politicians generally have confidently evoked it for most of this century. Western novels, though no longer maintaining the extraordinary output of the years between the two World Wars, retain an enthusiastic readership for a formula with few variations. The Western film has been the single most popular film genre produced by Hollywood; estimates vary, but perhaps a total of 7,000 Westerns have been made since the first true narrative Western, the *Great Train Robbery* in 1903. By the early 1980s it was usual to hear that the Western movie was dead – film critic Pauline Kael had said it as early as 1974; ouput in the 1990s suggests the funeral was premature. The dominance of Western series on TV in the 1950s and 1960s (48 in 1959) was a significant cultural phenomenon; it is worth noting at least one cable station in the U.S. is still devoted exclusively to Westerns. Even if films and television are set aside, one test remains for the residual vitality of the appeal of the West: advertisers continue to rely confidently on its magnetic effect. This did not begin with Leo Burnett's invention of Marlboro Man in 1954. Western ikons sold whiskey, tobacco and canned foods from the 1870s, and a century later their general use, which now included everything from automobiles to cosmetics, coincided with a boom in

Western fashion clothes. In 1990 Budweiser's campaign put beer back on the range.

Perhaps most interesting, the image of the West has reached beyond the United States to other cultures, other nations who have not shared America's historical and cultural determinants - and generated a sympathetic and enthusiastic response. That image, and the beliefs which underpin it, are, in the precisest use of the term, a modern myth.

Chapter Two

Myths And Heroes

The story of the West is our Trojan War, our Volsunga Saga, our Arthurian cycle, our Song of Roland.

Thomas K. Whipple, 1943

In the end, myths become part of the language, as a deeply encoded set of metaphors that may contain all the "lessons" we have learned from our history, and all the crucial elements of our world view.

Richard Slotkin, 1975

Sooner or later, virtually everyone who has written about the West refers to 'the myth.' Forty-five years ago Henry Nash Smith subtitled *Virgin Land,* his seminal study on nineteenth-century popular ideas about the West, *The American West in Symbol and Myth.* Robert G. Athearn chose to call his summation of sixty years' thinking about the West's history *The Mythic West.* Bernard de Voto identified collective popular attitudes to the West as not only the most enduring but the finest of America's myths. Russell Martin has entitled his uncritically affectionate review of the evolution of the cowboy *The Enduring Myth of the Wild West.* Joe B. Frantz and Julien E. Choate in *The American Cowboy: the Myth and the Reality* aver 'the range rider is a myth, but he is a myth possessing a living and present reality in the American folk mind.' Western fiction, writes James K. Folsom, reiterates a 'myth or fable.' Will Wright has analysed the Western film as a vehicle for a modern functional myth. Linking movies and history, Jenni Calder begins by saying: 'The West is loaded with myth.' This list could be extended indefinitely. The difficulty is, few of those who use the term (with the exception of Wright) give much idea of precisely what they mean by 'myth.'

None of these writers is implying that the received wisdom on the West is some sort of popular fallacy, or a general falsification of the historical record. (Even if this were so, it would not make the United States remarkable – most nations have at some point adjusted their past, usually to justify the present.) When writers on the West refer to myth, they usually mean something else entirely: they intend an analogy with the great stories of the older cultures. As Thomas K. Whipple put it, 'The story of the West is our Trojan War, our Volsunga Saga, our Arthurian cycle, our song of Roland' – epic tales of gods and heroes, struggles and quests. Why, one might well ask, should Americans want a Homeric version of their history? Carl Sonnichsen suggests that it all grows out of 'a natural and normal hunger for a heroic past,' arguing that 'Any group with a thousand-year history has these things provided, but the American is a new-comer and not yet completely at home in his vast country. All he has is the mythical West, and he needs it desperately.'

This is difficult to take seriously. For a start, the argument that the Western myth is a response to a national yearning for a tradition is circular: it springs from the deep-seated American belief that a new and unique culture emerged in the United States. But *that* belief is itself part of the Western myth – that what made America unique was exemplified in the conquest of the West. More important, for the last century-and-a-half Americans have demonstrably *not* been seeking a tradition. Foreign observers, like Alexis de Tocqueville, from the early days of the Republic were constantly to comment on this. At the end of the century, prominent Americans agreed. William Dean Howells remarked in 1897: 'There is no past for us, only the future.' Eleven years later, back from a twenty-year exile, Henry James wrote: 'What was taking place was a perpetual repudiation of the past, so far as there is a past to repudiate.' Americans seemed to have taken Ralph Waldo Emerson's advice, when he argued back in 1836 that they should reject history and take only nature and expe-rience as guides. There were perfectly good reasons for this attitude. Everything in America seemed new; the problems were new, there were no precedents, so the past had no valid lessons to offer – as Abraham Lincoln put it: 'As our case is new, so we must think anew, and act anew.' Moreover, the pace of change was recognised as extraordinary, so that tradition, desirable or not, was irrelevant. James Fenimore Cooper (first literary creator of the Western hero) in 1838 spoke for each succeeding generation when he said: 'We are a nation of change.'

Nevertheless, the story of the conquest of the West is persistently spoken of as if it were like the stories of ancient and tribal cultures which explain how the world got to be the way it is. This makes it the sort of myth which, Mircea Elaide tells us, '...narrates a sacred history; it relates an event that took place in a primordial time, the fabled time of the "beginnings."' In her justly acclaimed study of the West, *The Legacy of Conquest*, Patricia Nelson Limerick affirms that 'every human group has a creation myth,' which she defines as 'a tale explaining where its members came from and why they are special, chosen by providence for a special destiny,' to which white Americans are no exception for 'their most popular origin myth concerns the frontier.'

This reads too much like another version of the yearning-for-tradition argument. Setting aside what Professor Limerick means by a 'human group,' the fact is that, as the anthropologists would recognise such a concept, no post-primitive society has produced an origin myth. Why should it? New societies emerging in the last several hundred years are the products of political transformations of one sort or another, and they are therefore heirs to long-standing cultural and social forces. For the United States, the time of the 'beginnings' as a nation was the Revolution and white Americans know where their origins lie – they came from Europe. A nation may at some point conceive a sense of specific purpose (*la mission civilisatrice française*, the vanguard of international communism), rhetoric may proclaim it a destiny and history adjusted to support it. But such ideas remain in the realm of propaganda and political slogans. Taking its cue from Professor Limerick, a recent summary of revisionist histories of the West in *U.S. News & World Report* began: 'It is our Book of Genesis. Our legend of Romulus and Remus. The story of the frontier is America's myth of creation.' It is not. And present-day Italians, citizens of a nation-state born a century after the U.S.A., are unlikely to think much about Romulus and Remus; American Christians and Jews still have the Book of Genesis.

If the great story of the West is not a creation myth, what kind is it? For myth is not a term to be used lightly: its study is an academic battleground. Why societies generate myths and exactly what purpose they serve has been a matter of no small conflict among anthropologists, psychologists, sociologists and literary analysts. It is not yet clear who is winning and non-combatants enter this battle zone at their peril. Consensus accepts that myths have functions beyond explaining origins. Bronislav Malinowski says of tribal societies that 'Myth fulfils in primitive culture an indispensable function: it expresses, enhances and codifies belief: it vouches for the efficiency of ritual and contains practical rules for the guidance of man.'

Primitive myths thus serve as a vehicle for transmitting to each generation what the society believes is essential to the way it works, including its values. It does this symbolically through stories, and a great deal of attention has been devoted to the narrative structure of myths, in part to understand their origins. However the myth-stories originate – and debate on the problem continues to flourish – some of them do appear to derive from history, that is to say, myths take bits of history and turn them into legends which illustrate the force of the myth's central ideas. They also seize on legends which have arisen quite independently; like the gravity-well of giant stars, myths pull in elements wandering in local space and absorb them.

It is tempting to use all this as a description for the myth of the West. In America, a set of past experiences became a model for the present and future because Americans chose to see in them something crucial. Over time, stories illustrating those experiences were turned, through endless repetition, into legends which became unchallengeable because they 'proved' the propositions of the myth. The themes of the myth percolated into society until they ended up as conventions, universally accepted. Thus Richard Slotkin, in the introduction to his own version of the Western myth, argues: 'In the end, myths become part of the language, as a deeply encoded set of metaphors that may contain all the "lessons" we have learned from our history, and all the crucial elements of our world view.'

A problem with this argument is that many of the anthropologists insist that myths exist only in primitive societies. Primitive man has myths, we are told, because he does not have a recorded history to explain the past nor science to explain the world. On this basis myths, we would assume, disappear as a society becomes more sophisticated, becomes 'modern.' Currently however one of the more fashionable ways of looking at myths in primitive cultures, deriving from the work of, among others, the anthropologist Claude Levi-Strauss, offers a different perspective. This view sees myths as performing a specific and very important function: they are a way of dealing with the conflicts societies produce for their members. Such conflicts might be as simple as the clash between human desires and social rules, or as complicated as a rift between the ideals of religion and the practicalities of experience. Thus stories of struggles and quests, gods and heroes act out the conflicts symbolically. Whatever the conflicts may be, if they are rooted deep in the culture, myths will emerge to provide reassurance.

If this is valid for primitive cultures, it is difficult to see why it should not be equally so for modern ones. Societies with a perfectly well-developed sense of history and an analytical approach to understanding the physical world seem to go on producing elaborate stories to explain away their conflicts. In such cases, with all due respect to the anthropologists, we might as well call them myths. They are most likely to arise as a means of dealing with a fundamental contradiction which compromises the core-values of the society, the sort of conflict which causes a persistent dilemma in the collective unconscious. There is in fact a spectacular example of exactly this sort of functional myth, one which lasted four hundred years in European culture and whose themes are still entirely familiar – the Arthurian myth.

The Arthur of history is hidden in mists like those which closed around the craft which carried the Arthur of legend to Avalon. The basis for medieval beliefs about this sixth-century figure was a mixture of legends and folktales and poems. But from the early twelfth century to the late fifteenth the Arthur story was taken up, elaborated, and structured until it was the myth of the age. This was certainly remarkable but is not inexplicable. By the twelfth century, European society faced a serious problem. The feudal warrior class, originally raised to defend the realm, was now privileged, idle, quarrelsome, armed and dangerous. To bring it under some form of social control, chivalry was invented. But to reprogram the warrior class more was needed than a code of conduct; what was required was a vivid and compelling example, validated by history. The Arthurian legends were ready and waiting to be adapted to this purpose. So twelfth-century English chroniclers, like Geoffrey of Monmouth, purporting to write history, produced the mighty king who founded a new order of knights. Thirteenth-century French poets added the Holy Grail quest and then the Round Table. Other stories, which had arisen far apart in time and place, were sucked in, like those of Gawaine, Tristan and Iseult, and Percival. At the end of the fifteenth century, Thomas Malory recombined all these elements into a single great version.

Something more has to explain the extraordinary potency and vitality of the Arthurian cycle than its use as a back-up for chivalry. Of course, the subject matter was romantic and escapist and attracted medieval writers who were looking for a subject for vernacular literature. It had clear political uses. Geoffrey of Monmouth's twelfth-century version was a deliberate attempt to create for post-Norman Conquest England a great and unified past to lend prestige to an upstart dynasty. The myth offered an idealised blueprint for feudal kingship (Edward III had his model for the Order of the Garter); fourteen years after Malory had written his comprehensive version, Caxton published it – no accident then that Henry VII, with a shaky claim to the throne he had seized in 1485, should promptly name his son Arthur as a crude piece of propaganda. But these are secondary effects – Arthur's name was a talisman because people believed the myth.

More important than all these was the myth's ability to touch a great contradiction at the heart of medieval society: a religion which enjoined peace and a rejection of worldly rewards and a political and social structure which encouraged neither. The myth presented a great tragedy: Camelot is destroyed by a cancer, born of human weakness, and the quest for the Holy Grail does not save it. Just as the noble promise of the Arthurian new order founders on men's inability to live up to their ideals, so medieval society feared the gulf between its ideals and its practice. Yet the myth was an invention. Its creators took a piece of the past and peopled it with characters who exemplified the qualities the *present* wanted to see. It dragged in other legends and made them serve the same purpose. Above all, its creators cut the stories free from the sixth century of history and set them in a *timeless* world, so that the myth could be re-interpreted again and again in images of the present.

The story of the conquest of the West, as it had emerged by the first decade of the twentieth century, was precisely the same sort of myth. It was not a creation story, nor was it the American version of Homer. Like the Arthurian myth, its raw material lay in fragments of history and accumulated legends, it was fuelled by writers seeking a vernacular literature and a public seeking escapism. It was legitimated by historians and turned to immediate political uses. But it was invented out of a need to solve a great cultural dilemma, a fundamental conflict between tenaciously held ideals and a reality which defied them. This conflict emerged in the last quarter of the nineteenth century and had become critical by 1890.

The idea of the West had always been involved in a special relationship with the American dream – that belief in the good society, in a special mission and in a destiny unique among nations. The dream began with the Puritans' faith that their covenant with God would guarantee their escape from the cyclic rise and fall of all previous societies in history, a fate consequent on man's sinfulness. They would escape it provided they kept their society simple and pure. This faith merged into a political creed a century-and-a-half later for those who founded the new nation: through its great experiment in republican government America would escape the evils which were ingrained in the Old World – laws and institutions which enshrined privilege, a society which rested on class-distinction and a civilisation decadent and corrupt.

The Republic of Virtue could not rest only on pious intentions and the Constitution. Fortunately providence had endowed the United States with a fail-safe factor – an empty continent. Thomas Jefferson explained: free land meant free men, westward expansion guaranteed the spread of a property-owning democracy, a society dominated by yeoman farmers, independent of means and therefore of judgment. Others saw that it offered further advantages: it would drain the poor and discontented from the crowded East and it would provide an immense supply of cheap food from an agricultural heartland. The Great West was America's guarantee of her special destiny. By the 1840s that destiny had become 'manifest,' a pre-ordained expansion westward. The power of these theories as propaganda was in inverse proportion to their relevance to the real world. Jefferson's free farmers fought to enter the market economy, where naturally, like everyone else, they became prisoners of market forces. The frontier was never a real safety-valve for the urban poor (most lacked the capital and knowhow for Western farming) and plenty of contemporaries feared that 'manifest destiny' was a cover for imperialism.

The nature of the West itself was for some time a matter of debate. For example, what effect did life in the wilderness have on those who chose it? One view had long claimed that contact with the wilderness inevitably depraved human beings until, without the restraints of civilised society, they became as savage as the beasts among whom they dwelt. On the other hand, ideas stretching back to biblical roots held that the wilderness purified and redeemed where civilisation ultimately corrupted. This notion had taken on new force with Rousseau's paeans of praise for the life of nature and had become an article of faith for the Romantic movement. By the mid-nineteenth century its most influential spokesman in America was Henry Thoreau, though many writers had persistently argued that only in the wilderness could the pristine virtues flourish. This obviously fitted neatly with the political value of the West: it was a moral and spiritual resource as well as a vital national asset. Needless to say, those who advocated these theories did not practise them; even Thoreau carefully interspersed his ostentatiously simple life in his cabin at Walden Pond with quick trips back to the city for civilised company.

The trans-Mississippi West posed the geographical equivalent of this debate. Early exploration, like the expeditions of Lieutenant Zebulon Pike in 1805-6 and Major Stephen Long in 1819-20, believed it had found the Great American Desert. Of the Plains, Long wrote: 'I do not hesitate in giving the opinion, that it is almost wholly uninhabitable by a people depending on agriculture for their subsistence.' This bleak vision was dispelled by later explorers and the settlers who followed them from the 1840s. By the 1870s it had been replaced by the equally fallacious but potentially more dangerous idea that the West would prove a vast and bounteous garden of plenty.

The prevailing viewpoint eventually came to see the settlement of the West as one of the most dramatic proofs of America's commitment to 'progress.'

For the vast majority of Americans who felt no urge to migrate into the wilderness, watching the conquest of the West allowed a smug patriotic satisfaction because it apparently demonstrated progress in action. This attitude was visible as early as the 1780s, when settlers spilled over the Appalachians into the Ohio Valley, and just increased with time. In an age before mass entertainment, the frontier was also the best spectator sport available. Journalists seeking subjects to illustrate the great march of progress, often followed by writers of heroic biographies, produced men they, not history, selected to lead that advance. Popular writers also turned to the West. The success of the novels of James Fenimore Cooper in the 1820s and 1830s encouraged a torrent of cheap adventure stories in the next two decades; with the advent of dime novels after 1860 the torrent became a flood.

In his famous analysis of the United States, written in the late 1830s, Alexis de Tocqueville thought, because the new nation was recording history as it was being made, the American past would never be cluttered with legends. For once his insight failed him, for here he underestimated the American ingenuity he admired. Both journalists and fiction-writers took real-life figures and turned them into creatures of fantasy. Inevitably, it became impossible to separate reality from make-believe, even if an eager public had the slightest interest in doing so. Journalistic excess was credited as truth, repetition turned stories into folktales, wish-fulfilment made legends. Not centuries after their death, but within their lifetimes Daniel Boone was the torchbearer of civilisation in the wilderness, Kit Carson a superhuman scout and Jesse James the American Robin Hood.

Thus from the beginning of the new nation an extraordinary complex of ideas about the West was imbedded in nineteenth-century Americans' thinking about themselves and their future. On this ground, it might well be thought that these ideas amounted to a myth in their own right. Indeed, Henry Nash Smith, whose *Virgin Land* first really opened up this subject, has unhesitatingly said that they did. But he defined myth as 'an intellectual construction that fuses concept and emotion into an image.' This is a convenient umbrella under which to group a lot of popular notions which, as Smith emphasised, 'sometimes exert a decided influence on practical affairs.' But on that basis any widely held cluster of ideas and images qualifies as a myth and from there it is only a short step to Roland Barthes's unhelpful remark that anything can become a myth.

If myths are seen in terms of the function they perform, a different picture emerges. America's thinking about the West for most of the nineteenth century was a mixture of half-baked philosophy and political theory, enlivened with folktales and literary fantasy. These notions related to a continuing process: the role of the West in maintaining social stability and guaranteeing 'progress.' The block of ideas which appeared at the century's end were quite different. These took as their starting point the belief that the traditional role of the West was finished, and that this in itself was a tragedy. They concentrated not on the long story of successive settlements of the West, but on one – and recent – episode, the cattleman's frontier. The basic intention of these ideas, like the Arthurian stories, was to look *back* for a model for action – they looked to the past to redeem the future.

This would suggest that the new construct grew out of a widely-held perception that something had gone dreadfully wrong with the present. It is in fact easy to demonstrate that the *myth* of the West arose out of a crisis which exposed a contradiction at the heart of America's self-image. In the thirty-five years following the end of the Civil War, a huge industrial economy emerged, cities mushroomed and immigration added 11 million to a population which doubled in size to 75 million. Such growth brought problems: unregulated business exploitation of the market, vast disparities of wealth, violent labour disputes. Particularly alarming was an agricultural depression which brought farmers, including those in the West, to organised political protest. To the paranoia which lurks never too far beneath the surface of American political thinking, the Republic of Virtue was under siege from within, the American dream was turning into a nightmare.

Of course, most of this was just an exaggerated reaction, faced sooner or later by all modern societies, to the implications of becoming an urban-industrial nation. But other modern societies were not stuck with America's value system. The real crisis was in the minds of many Americans, who saw a frightening conflict between how they conceived their country and what it had become. All the evils which characterised the wicked old world, which the United States had so confidently expected to escape, seemed to have re-emerged. Yet American core-values were enshrined in agrarian idealism –

self-reliant individualism had underpinned the structure of government and the political process. These values had encouraged laissez-faire policies, a rejection of the need for welfare legislation and suspicion of the role of government in general. But now these values seemed irrelevant: only the power of the state seemed able to hold disruptive forces in check, forces which were beyond the control of the individual. The many Americans who thought like this were filled with nostalgia for another America, where things were simple, and life uncorrupted and free.

In former decades, optimists would have looked to the West as the magic escape route from the impending disaster. But the old fail-safe factor had proved to have built-in obsolescence. It did not need the Census Report of 1890 to announce that the frontier was, in effect, closed: it had become obvious that the days of limitless free land were over. Besides, the West was already irretrievably shaped by the same forces which were contaminating the rest of the nation and was suffering from a major agricultural depression. This in itself had yet more alarming implications: if the old logic was correct, progress had brought its own nemesis – the advance of civilisation had destroyed the purifying power of the wilderness.

In essence, America appeared to be faced with the choice of rejecting a future which her own commitment to progress had wrought, or abandoning her value system. The smart move at this juncture would have been to meet the future with pragmatism, not an outworn creed. Since however nations do not usually junk their value systems with a shrug of the shoulders, nor give up economic growth by choice, this dilemma cried out for a myth to resolve it. It seems inevitable from today's standpoint that this myth should be centred on the West. Not the real West of the 1890s of course – that was not a solution, it was part of the problem – but a West of the imagination. The reasons for this are not difficult to detect.

For a start, Americans had been saturated with images of a land where the borderline between fact and fantasy was as unclear as the frontier between savagery and civilisation, so just about anything might be believed about the West. Then, nostalgia for the lost wilderness and the end of the frontier became bound up with nostalgia for a simpler America. This did not happen by accident: it was engineered by a handful of key figures each of whom was a deliberate and self-conscious myth-maker. They focussed attention not on the West in general, but on the last, most recent frontier and, ignoring everything which did not fit their inspiring vision, they portrayed it as the arena where all the old values fuelled heroic endeavour – a world of chivalry, honour, courage and self-reliance. This inspired propaganda was made respectable, even while it was being produced, by an historical hypothesis which confirmed what the propagandists had implied: that the frontier experience had permanently shaped the American character. This was particularly good news, for it meant that the *idea* of the West was immortal. In effect, the myth-makers had said: 'There. In that place and that time, it was the way it should be. Now it is gone for ever. But all is not lost. We carry within us its spirit, so it will continue to flourish if we let it. Now all we have to do is to go on retelling the story to keep us on the right track.'

All this obviously has some striking similarities with the Arthurian myth – a noble era, its tragic loss, a model for action. And neither of course grew naturally out of the fertile soil of the folk-mind, as one supposes ancient and tribal myths did – both were deliberately invented. Of course, the first medieval myth-makers reached back six hundred years for their material; they called up shadow history, their protagonists, if indeed they had ever existed historically, had outlines so fluid they could be reshaped at will. This left the inventors confident that their inventions were pretty safe from direct challenge. The first American myth-makers were trawling a past scarcely more than a decade old, so the history of the West was still being written when the myth began. Their protagonists therefore had substance (a great many were still alive!), yet they unhesitatingly wove a fabric of fantasy. Moreover, the creators were for the most part not Westerners – from start to finish the West of myth was invented by the East. On any sensible assumptions this should have meant the myth died stillborn – but instead of challenging the fantasies, the real West enthusiastically subscribed to them.

In general, Americans as myth-makers showed a good deal of ingenuity. The medieval writers took a realm facing chaos and gave it an order of chivalrous knights to show the future how peace and harmony might reign. Americans took the problems of getting cattle to market and a class of agricultural labourers as the role models for the generations to come. The speed with which the Western myth took hold is testimony to American knowhow. The Arthurian myth began in the twelfth century, and it developed over four hundred years; the Western myth began in the 1890s and was in definitive form in twenty. It had however certain advantages. Images of a fantasy West had been broadcast by modern media – newspapers and a publishing revolution which created mass-produced literature. And from the start the Western myth received its biggest impetus from showbusiness. Medieval peasants, if they could escape for a moment from the crushing drudgery of their daily round, might sneak a glimpse of chivalry in action at a tournament. In the last fifteen years of the nineteenth century, *millions* of Americans saw the pageant of the frontier in Buffalo Bill's Wild West. Above all the Western myth had the cinema. The film industry seized on the myth, amplified it and added to it.

The crisis of the 1890s which produced the myth eventually, in the natural course of events, faded away. The myth, obviously, did not. Some of the reasons for this are fairly clear. In the 1920s and 1930s it looked as if it had become tied to the business cycle – the myth flourished in the decade of prosperity and waned in the Depression. In actuality it had suffered an inevitable fate: it had become locked into politics. It was appropriated, in the name of self-reliant individualism, by those who for their own motives were defending laissez-faire and remained to be invoked by those who claimed the nation's health rested on roll-back of the power of government – as Ronald Reagan amply demonstrated. But this was only possible because echoes of the myth never ceased to reverberate in the nation's unconscious, for each new set of problems tested the American Dream, and the Dream was shored up by the myth. A piece of insignificant history had been given an awesome role: the trick had been to change the West into a timeless world on which images of the present could be endlessly reimposed. As numberless public figures were to say, from the prototype cowboy film star Tom Mix to the poet Archibald MacLeish, the West became a country of the mind.

Chapter Three

Manufacturing Images

That thar might be true but I hain't got no reckerlection of it.

Kit Carson, on being shown the cover of
a novel featuring him in heroic pose.

The Only Real Novelty of the Century. The Amusement
Triumph of the Age. The Romantic West Brought East in
Reality.

Press release for Buffalo Bill's Wild West, 1887

The West was where anything could happen. For most of the nineteenth century it was a land of infinite possibility, not because its immense resources could be exploited with ease – it was soon found they could not – but because it was a stage on which some of the nation's more important dreams could be focussed. No matter what the real West was like, it was invested with qualities, attributes, inhabitants and events which were largely the products of imagination. Partly this was because it just stayed remote. Despite their interest and pride in it, the West was where most Americans chose not to live. True for the nineteenth century, this is still true: the tier of states bisected by the Continental Divide, Arizona, New Mexico, Utah, Colorado, Idaho, Wyoming and Montana, has today a combined population not much larger than New York City. It was also because a West of the imagination was packaged and marketed by four generations of astute image-makers, playing on public gullibility for their own ends. Americans were sold the idea that the conquest of the wilderness was the visible proof of their commitment to progress, of their manifest destiny, of their unique society.

To this extent the conquest of the West provided moral and patriotic satisfaction and escapism in much the same way that the Empire did for the British. From armchair comfort, the Victorian public admired the advance of 'dominion over palm and pine' and congratulated themselves on taking up the white man's burden. The Empire was also a constant arena for vicarious excitement. The conquest of distant lands and their savage inhabitants became standard fare for adventure stories and, when projected eventually by the yellow press, stimulated what one contemporary called 'spectatorial lust.' Some parts of the Empire, like darkest Africa, were still being explored late in the century and were therefore fair game for the imagination. Who knew what might be found in the interior? The gorilla was first brought to the notice of the outside world in 1847 (by an American missionary). When H. Rider Haggard published *King Solomon's Mines* in 1885, it was still possible that Africa might contain an unknown tribe of fierce warriors, complete with hideous customs and sitting on a diamond mine.

But the West was only very briefly darkest America. In 1800 knowledge of the whole area west of the Mississippi was extremely vague. It was not an unknown land, for it had been penetrated and traversed by Spaniards, French Canadians and agents of the British Hudson's Bay Company – it was just unknown to Americans. (Native Americans of course knew it very well indeed.) Shortly before President Jefferson dispatched Lewis and Clark to explore the Louisiana Purchase of 1803, the skeleton of a prehistoric mastodon had been discovered in upstate New York. Since no current scientific theory held the possibility that creatures could become extinct, it was not unreasonable then to suppose that the unknown West might contain roving herds of mastodon. Yet long after government-sponsored explorations, like the expeditions of Lewis and Clark in 1804-6, Pike in 1805-7, Long in 1820, after the fur trappers had explored the Rockies and found the routes to the Pacific shore, even after John Charles Frémont in the 1840s stole the trappers' credit and publicised himself as The Pathfinder, the West remained mysterious. Settlement did not change this much. There were sufficient Americans in Oregon by 1846 for the United States to push Britain into accepting a boundary at the 49th. parallel, the Mormons founded Salt Lake City in 1847, miners had chased strikes in Colorado and Nevada in 1858. But their experiences did not become a part of public knowledge to the point where they took on a humdrum familiarity. The West was not a place but a set of ideas.

Two of those ideas, mutually contradictory, engendered a serious debate for much of the first half of the century, when settlement spilled over the Appalachian Mountains into the first West of Kentucky, Tennessee and the Ohio Valley. Was the West the savage land, to be tamed so that civilisation could maintain its ordained progress across the continent? Or was it a vital spiritual resource, a land of freedom uncorrupted by the moral decadence that civilisation brings? The cultural historian Henry Nash Smith has drawn attention to how profoundly ambivalent attitudes to the frontier were – but it is well to ask, who held these attitudes? Certainly not Westerners, who simply saw themselves pursuing opportunity and besides, frontier settlers were utilitarians who despised theorising. Publishers found that in the West there was very little interest in books about the frontier – a trend that was to continue until the 1880s – and literacy in the West was much lower than in the East; fewer than 4% of the population of Kentucky were receiving a school education in 1840. The debate about the West was largely conducted by writers and intellectuals, most of them Easterners. The authors who saw the spirit of Rousseau striding about the West in buckskins and carrying a long rifle were affecting a fashionable romantic pose. Eastern readers pretending sophistication presumably brooded about the implications; others, reflecting national optimism and simply seeking escapist literature, were less interested in philosophical conjecture than in the pageant of the Westward advance.

That advance was not presented as an anonymous tide: it was personified by figures who were given special status. Out of the West ultimately came America's most durable heroes. When shorter-lived enthusiasms had faded, permanent heroic status was not given to Revolutionary War patriots, Southern cavaliers, intrepid Yankee skippers, penniless immigrants who became millionaire entrepreneurs, or men of the people who went from log cabin to White House – though each of these had his day and all embodied some aspect of America's beliefs about herself. It was the Western hero who found the widest appeal and showed the most consistent vitality. Yet those who actually *settled* the West failed to qualify. The pioneer farmers, whose enterprise marked the arrival of civilisation, the victors of the conquest, had only lip-service paid to their achievement. The heroes were those who preceded the farmers, blazed the trails and brought the frontier perils to manageable levels. Simply to be out in the wilderness was not enough: the true frontier heroes were nobly performing a socially useful task. Or at least, that is how they were presented. In actuality, the real-life figures chosen were invariably helpless pawns in the hands of propagandists for a particular image of the West.

Since the first frontier to be tamed was the trans-Appalachian forests, the first heroic frontier-tamer was the forest hunter. Daniel Boone was elected as the exemplar. Boone had been one of the explorers of Kentucky in the early 1770s, he had guided some settlers there in 1775 and helped defend the new settlements against Indian attacks in the Revolutionary War. He later moved twice more within Kentucky, then to what is now West Virginia and finally to Missouri. In 1784 John Filson wrote a history of Kentucky, mainly with the intention of attracting the attention of investors so that his own schemes might flourish, and appended a biography of Boone portraying him as the standard-bearer of civilisation in the wilderness. The only standard Boone had carried was that of the Transylvania Company, the notorious group of land speculators who hoped to make a quick killing in Kentucky. Then newspapers became fascinated by his frequent moves and typed him as that peculiar kind of frontiersman who so hated being crowded that he resettled as soon as he could see the smoke from his neighbour's chimney. Eastern Romantics translated this into the more noble figure who sought a life in nature, uncorrupted by civilisation. The reason why Boone made a career of moving on was his incompetence: he simply failed to register his land claims in Kentucky and West Virginia, so was legally ejected; he even failed to convert the Spanish grant he was given in Missouri and only after protracted appeals was it confirmed by Congress six years before his death in 1820.

By that point, thanks largely to the press, this obscure pioneer was a nationally-known figure. Byron had picked up on the Romantic implications – of course – and given Boone a eulogy in *Don Juan*, proudly quoted in the United States after the poem's publication in 1823. Ten years later Boone was the subject of a full biography by Timothy Flint. A New Englander who had settled in Cincinnati, Flint had two enthusiasms: he was a romantic idealist about 'nature' and an indefatigable propagandist for Western settlement. Not surprisingly therefore his Boone is simultaneously both fleeing civilisation and leading its advance. The reading public were presumably unworried by this inherent contradiction, for the book went through fourteen editions and is credited with being the most widely-read biography in America up to 1850. In 1860 Boone's canonisation was completed when George Bancroft, America's most influential historian before Turner, cast Boone in Volume VIII of his magisterial *History of the United States* as the saviour of the nation by leading her into a secure democratic future in the West. From start to finish, the poor man had greatness thrust upon him and at each stage he was stamped with other men's images of the West.

Immortality in another form awaited. James Fenimore Cooper's vastly popular Leatherstocking Tales, five novels published between 1823 and 1841, had as their central character a wilderness hunter who was meant to personify frontier virtues. Most authorities agree that though Cooper did not exactly base Leatherstocking on Boone, he had him in mind. Cooper's readers fused Boone and Leatherstocking together to produce a nationally-accepted image of the Western hero. He was the buckskin-clad, dead-shot hunter, with uncanny knowledge of the wilderness. His antagonists were Indians, who kidnapped white maidens, who in turn had to be rescued. Indians were devious, ruthless, evil and a barbaric barrier to civilisation's advance, so deserved slaughter, except for the occasional good Indian who proved himself the white man's loyal friend. Above all, the frontier hero of literature remained the outsider, unable to fit into civilised society and, often as not, he didn't get the girl. This model was to have a great future.

Cooper did not portray all Indians as villains but his readers knew that each advance westward had been bought at the cost of a bitter conflict with redskins. Five years after Boone had left for Missouri, Indian resistance north and west of the Ohio was broken by frontier riflemen under 'Mad Anthony' Wayne at the battle of Fallen Timbers: Cooper had Leatherstocking serve under Wayne. Even as Cooper was writing, Illinois and Wisconsin were made safe for settlement by the Black Hawk War of 1832. It has been claimed that *Last of the Mohicans* was the most widely read American novel of the nineteenth century; it is also the novel in which Cooper's Mingoes are portrayed as fundamentally evil and are attacked by Leatherstocking with the warcry 'Extarminate 'em!' Henceforward the frontier hero would have one primal function. Whether he was fleeing civilisation or leading its advance, he was an Indian-killer.

Though Easterners admired the great march into the wilderness, they did not particularly admire the society which sprang up in the West. On the contrary, Eastern snobbery made the crudity of Western life the butt of endless jokes. The West had also become well-known as the source of a new kind of American humour, wonderful anecdotes of exaggeration usually called 'tall tales.' Regarding tall tales as crude nonsense and the boasting as crass, the East tended to write off Westerners as uncouth, loud-mouthed braggarts. One man came to personify these traits: Davy Crockett.

Crockett the hero – King of the Wild Frontier as the 1954 hit-song put it – was not a product of legend. Nor was he the creation of nineteenth-century writers and the public imagination. Crockett the frontier superman, coonskin cap, buckskin shirt, homespun wisdom and awe-inspiring bravery, was invented in his entirety by the media in the 1950s. For a few brief years this Crockett was a national craze. A three-part TV series was turned in 1955 into a very successful film, which then had two sequels. Seizing on his potential, manufacturers then turned Crockett into a marketing device, so that his name endorsed an extraordinary range of products. None of this was based on history, nor on legends, nor folktales (even the song was specially written for the TV series). This Crockett was a media artifact, the product of a search for a variant on the frontier theme in a decade which produced more Western films than any before it. The Crockett of history had enjoyed a different kind of fame.

In the nineteenth century, Crockett's fame had been brief as a politician who had played the theme tune of the Age of Jackson – the common man who makes good. He was portrayed as the astute yokel who defeated his opponents by low cunning and frontier humour; his death at the Alamo did not transform this image. Never known as an Indian-killer, as a backwoods hunter he eventually became bracketed with Boone – Theodore Roosevelt was a founder member of a group of gentleman-sportsmen interested in conservation who called themselves the Boone and Crockett Club. As a frontier humourist Crockett survived in a different way through the 'Crockett Almanacks,' cheap prints which retold and embellished old frontier tall tales and added new ones. Entirely appropriately, as a master of the tall tale himself, Crockett was turned by the Almanacks into a comic giant of fable – but they left no basis for a national hero of flesh and blood. Except, that is, in Texas. There, where the revolution against Mexico approaches the status of a creation myth and the martyrs of the Alamo are near-sacred figures, Crockett remained revered. The reverence continues undimmed. In 1978 some evidence emerged which suggested that Crockett had hidden throughout the siege and attempted to escape death by claiming he was an innocent bystander. Public uproar resulted, with one newspaper claiming the publication was a Communist plot.

By the time of Crockett's death in 1836, public attention had turned from the forests of Kentucky and Boone/Leatherstocking to a new West. In their vicarious quest for romance and excitement, Easterners persistently looked not to what was happening at the limits of settlement – that was just a risky variation of what many of them were doing themselves – but beyond to the cutting edge of the frontier. From the 1830s to the 1850s much excitement was generated by tales of the mountain men, the fur trappers of the Far West. It is difficult to exaggerate the exploits of the mountain men, even though many of them did their best to do so. Their courage, endurance and skills were of an extraordinary order. By the 1840s, the mountain man had become a new and exciting character in the great Western drama. He had been thrust on to the stage not by straightforward reporting of his remarkable activities, although good examples of such reporting existed. Writers seized on this new figure to manipulate his potential for illustrating the *idea* of the frontier. The fur trapper was fresh and wonderful copy to be exploited. What emerged followed the pattern already laid down for frontier heroes. Fact gleaned from stories, reports and travellers' accounts was reinterpreted through the prejudices of the author; 'autobiographies' and biographies were tailored for a public seeking sensationalism; and novels took up and extended the fiction already masquerading as truth. The mountain man was given a version of the same treatment which had produced the frontier-tamer of the forests.

The Eastern public did not however look on the achievements of the mountain men with the same admiration and moral approval in which Daniel Boone had basked. The image of the mountain man which had taken shape in the East by the 1840s was essentially that of a wild man, a solitary predator, rugged and brave, unwashed and illiterate, who threw away the profits of his herculean endeavours in annual orgies of drinking, gambling and general unmentionable profligacy. He was exciting and picturesque but he had three disturbing defects as hero-material. First was his symbiotic relationship with the Indians – most trappers were obliged to fight Indians part of the time, but some lived with Indians and some took Indian wives. Second, he had apparently deliberately rejected civilised society for the wrong reasons: he sought freedom in the wilderness not to exercise natural virtue but to enjoy himself free from society's rules. Third, he exemplified no great and noble purpose – collecting beaver pelts to make fashionable gentleman's headgear might be profitable but it was hardly the same as leading settlers into a new promised land.

These attitudes were unjust. In reality, there was no single type of mountain man. Some were illiterate, some not. Some indeed were loners, but the most effective trapping unit was the organised group called the brigade. Some threw away their desperately hard-earned profits to unscrupulous traders and in orgiastic release at the annual rendezvous, but others demonstrably did not. One interesting study has suggested that they should be seen simply as entrepreneurs in an entrepreneurial age; many just took their profits and went into other, safer and usually respectable occupations. More important, the mountain men had indeed made a crucial contribution to Western settlement. It was not government-sponsored expeditions which explored the Rockies and found the routes into Oregon and California, but trappers like Jedediah Smith, Jim Bridger, Thomas Fitzpatrick and Joseph Walker. Some indeed, like Smith and Zenas Leonard, saw the potential for settling the Pacific Shore.

But the mountain men were given little credit for their achievements and farsightedness at the time. The heyday of fur trapping was from the mid-1820s to the late 1830s; very suddenly, the fashion for beaver hats was replaced with one for the silk 'topper' and the trade simply collapsed – the last rendezvous was held in 1842. It is often forgotten that, though the East had seen some stories published about mountain men in the 1830s, the main rush of writing came from 1845 when to all intents and purposes the trade was over. The reason was simple. By that point the Far West was at the centre of political debate because ardent nationalists were pressing for the annexation of Oregon and California.

In the next thirty-five years, from about 1845 to 1880, Americans invented the Wild West. They polished, embellished and admired their invention and peopled it with inhabitants of their imagination. Shifting their gaze from the forests of Kentucky and Tennessee, now a part of history, and from the trappers of the Rocky Mountains, who were fading into a romantic episode, they looked to the whole frontier beyond the Mississippi as an arena for westward expansion and therefore for heroic drama.

In the great migration across the Mississippi into the new West which began after 1848, crossing the plains and mountains was as hazardous as ever. The physical barriers were formidable and the Indian menace acute, so that those who streamed out to Oregon and California needed guiding and the Army, embarked on a role of making the Plains safe, needed experts for reconnaissance. Both were promptly seen to be dependent on the scout – far seeing, wise in the ways of the wilderness, a deadly foe to the redskins. The only people available to fill this role were mountain men, many of whom, putting to obvious use their knowledge of the land and Indians, already had switched to acting as guides when the fur trade declined and the first attempts were made to find wagon trails to the Pacific shore. In terms of public acclaim, they got little credit for it until one of the obscurest of them was catapulted to fame.

The catalyst for that process, and a good deal else besides, was John Charles Frémont, soldier, explorer, politician and adventurer. Frémont's three expeditions to the Far West between 1842 and 1846 gave him the title of 'the Pathfinder' and a reputation as the greatest explorer of the age. Both were unearned. Frémont was a good scientific geographer and a competent map-maker; his major contribution to geographical knowledge was to identify the Great Basin and his major practical achievement was to convince those back East that the Plains were not a desert. He was credited with exploring the key routes through the Rockies and for leading the first wagon train west in 1843. He did neither: the mountain men had already found all the important routes and passes; one of them led the first wagons into California and a missionary led the first into Oregon.

Nevertheless, Frémont was a truly important figure because his greatest talent was for publicity. His official reports on the first two expeditions were masterpieces of vivid prose and when published in 1845 were instant best-sellers (they were reprinted seven times by 1856). Frémont caught the public imagination and directed it westward at the high point of the shrill cries about Manifest Destiny. With his involvement on the third expedition in the seizure of California at the outbreak of the Mexican War, he became a national figure and his influence was to last for a generation. Though Frémont judiciously distributed praise for services rendered by his guides, he reserved unstinting admiration for one of them – Kit Carson.

Born in 1809 in Kentucky and raised on the Missouri border, Carson had run away to New Mexico when he was seventeen and became a trapper three years later. He had made no particular name for himself but by 1840 was a seasoned mountain man. He met Frémont by accident in St. Louis in 1842 and became *one* of his guides on each of the three expeditions up to 1846. Frémont's reports over and over again praise Carson – 'my true and reliable friend' – for his skills, bravery and outstanding dependability. The ambitious Frémont was doubtless deliberately creating a heroic image for himself and another for Carson as his foil. During the Mexican War, in the conquest of California, Carson earned a considerable, indeed an excessive, reputation as a courier for Frémont and a guide to General Kearney's force on the last leg of its advance. An English naval officer, who met Carson at the end of the hostilities in California in 1846, wrote: 'Why, he is as famous here as is the Duke [of Wellington] in Europe,'* and when he finally went East to Washington in 1847 he was greeted with a hero's welcome.

Frémont had made Carson; as his fame rose so did Carson's until it eclipsed his creator's. By the time Frémont ran, unsuccessfully, for the presidency in 1856 his supporters were using Carson's name to shed lustre on their candidate. Carson had become a national figure: from that point he moved inexorably to become a legend. Henry Nash Smith and Kent L. Steckmesser have charted this voyage in detail. Reverent biographers produced a Carson unknown to his friends but entirely suited to his Eastern admirers: genteel, well-spoken (to the point of literary pedantry) and abstemious. No-one who knew him ever doubted Carson's courage, but his near-illiteracy,

---

* This was praise indeed, for the Post Office had become used to delivering letters to the Duke addressed merely 'No. 1, London.'

broad dialect (including the usual range of mountain man oaths), and liking for whiskey were just as obvious. Carson had been irrevocably set on the road that Daniel Boone had travelled before him. The final accolade came, five years after Carson's death, when in 1873 John S.C. Abbott included Carson in his series of biographies, 'American Pioneers and Patriots.' Abbott was a clergyman-turned-popular-historian, much acclaimed, with a reputation for combining drama with moral uplift in his writings.* Abbott's Carson is a pillar of moral rectitude as well as a model of chivalry.

Beyond the solemn biographies, Carson soon took on a new life in literature, appearing in novel after novel under his own name – but not of course as his real self. The Carson of fiction, particularly of the dime novels which flooded the market after 1860, took on whatever characteristics the writer believed best illustrated what he thought the public wanted to hear about the frontier. If the frontier hero was intended to be an edifying example, then the Carson of the biographies was displayed, but side by side with those predictable inventions another Carson emerged, savage, brutal – and an Indian-killer. It is usually implied that the wild and woolly Carson is as much an invention as the gentleman-scout. Certainly he usually grew at least four inches on the real Carson's five feet six and put on fifty pounds of herculean muscles. But this should not obscure the fact that Carson *was* an Indian-killer. Frémont's Reports are full of accounts of Carson's Indian fights and include, for April 1844, a detailed description of Carson killing and scalping two Indians, one of them while still alive. Boone is alleged to have admitted that he only killed one Indian in his whole career. With Carson's real record as a basis, it was entirely predictable that the prolific dime novelist Edward Ellis should eventually call him 'the most renowned Indian fighter the world ever produced.'

As a legendary hero, Carson pioneered a new trend which took him a great step beyond Boone. Those who wrote nonsense about Boone were writing what purported to be history; Cooper and his later imitators drew on actual persons and events but were writing romances (even if their readers made obvious connections); and the publishers of Crockett tall tales were perpetuating a comic tradition. Carson was unhesitatingly turned into fiction. The reason lies in America's developing attitude to the West: it was the land where anything was possible. By the 1840s, when tales of the mountain men had shown its inhabitants were extraordinary, the boundary – in the experience of the East – between the credible and the incredible had

* The author's copy was originally presented as a Sunday School prize in 1896

become blurred. Into that misty land, novelists thrust a character whose real exploits were beyond the comprehension of city-dwellers anyway. Carson, like all those who followed him down the road to fictional immortality, was unlikely to sue for libel!

Well before his death in 1868, for Carson himself fantasy and the real world became inextricably entangled. Two of the best-known stories about Carson bear repeating because they illustrate this process so well. In 1849 he was asked to guide a troop of dragoons in pursuit of a band of Apaches who had captured a white woman, a Mrs. J.M. White. The party arrived too late – the Indians had killed their captive and fled – but amid the abandoned loot in the Apache camp, lay a copy of a novel in which (of course) Carson rescues a white girl from fiendish redskins. Seventeen years later, Colonel Henry Inman (who eventually wrote several romantic accounts of his own experiences in the West) showed Carson a lurid illustration of a heroic Kit defending a white girl from a horde of red savages. Carson is reported to have said: 'That thar might be true but I hain't got no reckerlection of it.'

From the 1840s the public became saturated with images of the West through the emergence of true mass media. The decisive step was a publishing revolution, both in technology and marketing. Steam had powered printing presses in Britain since 1814, but the first successful rotary steam press, capable of printing 8,000 copies an hour, was patented in New York in 1845. Twenty years later, a method for running continuous rolls of paper (instead of single sheets) through a rotary press completed the technical changes needed for mass-circulation publishing. The rotary press did not merely benefit newspapers; it encouraged the rise of the weekly story paper emerging first in Boston and New York in the mid-1840s and reaching circulations of over 100,000 copies ten years later. Distribution received a major boost in 1857 when the Post Office dropped magazine mail charges to two cents. New and aggressive marketing techniques were adopted: the *New York Ledger* bought space for striking advertisements in rival papers and ran 'teaser' episodes of its stories in them, while Street and Smith, publishers of the *New York Weekly*, pioneered the use of billboards along railroad tracks and mobilised the hitherto ignored army of newsagents as salesmen. The huge demand for story papers was perceived to be in the main from young working girls. Street and Smith believed they detected an equal if not larger market among young men. They were right and they inaugurated a switch from predominantly sentimental hogwash to adventure hokum – and amid the subjects available the Wild West was a natural contender for a predominant place.

A further and decisive change in marketing took place in 1860. Irwin Beadle and his partner Robert Adams brought out the first of a series of novels in a simple all-paper format at a price of ten cents (half the cost of the equivalent in a story paper). The dime novel was launched. In 1862 Erastus Beadle bought out his brother Irwin but saw his employee George Munro set up a rival firm; more competitors emerged with Frank Tousey in 1878 and Street and Smith's late decision to issue dime novels in 1889. The publishers all took a similar line on the nature of the enterprise: they were marketing a product. Novels were standardised at a $75 – $150 payment for 35,000 words, with an initial print run of 60,000 copies. Beadle and Adams concentrated on packaging the product: authors were instructed on stock plots and characters and the magic of repeating the familiar. Street and Smith targeted their market and tailored their stories accordingly. The output of dime novels was stupendous: all told, up to their demise at different times in the twentieth century, Beadle and Adams produced twenty-five series, Frank Tousey thirty and Street and Smith fifty. It is difficult to separate out reprints, re-issues under new titles and other duplications, but up to the end of the century figures indicate Beadle and Adams had produced 3,688 issues, Munro 1,362, Frank Tousey 2,154 and Street and Smith 2,802.

The dime novel has been inseparably associated with the Wild West. It was, but not of course exclusively. Dime fiction covered every theme for stories of adventure, and followed rather than created trends – if a plot-line sold, it was instantly copied and recopied. Cooper-imitations were a stock item (Beadle's most successful issue was their eighth, Edward S. Ellis's *Seth Jones*, complete with Leatherstocking clone, which sold 600,000 copies) and they went on being produced up until the 1890s. Sea stories, cashing in on the world-wide success of Yankee trader-captains, were a craze in the 1870s and 1880s. Detective stories arrived earlier than might be supposed – Munro introduced 'Old Sleuth' in 1885 and Street and Smith gave the world the deathless Nick Carter in 1891. General adventure stories, usually involving the irresistible rise to fame (and often fortune) of poor-but-honest lads (and girls too), always formed a large part of the output.

The exact amount of dime fiction devoted to the West is difficult to estimate. It was clearly very large: Philip Durham has said two-thirds and Daryl Jones, in his excellent study of dime novel Westerns, suggests 75 per cent. This latter figure looks high even if one includes Cooper-imitations, essentially frontier-historical rather than Wild West. A survey of the surviving works of a handful of the best-known dime novel authors shows a good deal of variation. On the basis of titles still existing, Albert W. Aiken wrote about two-thirds of his novels on general Wild West themes, Joseph E. Badger about half, Edward S. Ellis about 45% and St. George Rathbone, prolific juvenile author, about 35%. Some of course specialised in the Wild West: three-quarters of William R. Eyster's output was set on the frontier and, naturally, so were 90% of the tales of 'Buckskin Sam' Hall, former Texas Ranger.

Nor were dime novels the first cheap outlet for tales of the new West: the story papers beat them to it by several years. Street and Smith led the way into turning the Wild West into a publishers' bonanza through the *New York Weekly*, which published the first of Edward Zane Carroll Judson's new Western stories in 1869. Judson had been a successful writer since 1846, mostly, though far from exclusively, of sea stories – hence his regular pseudonym of Ned Buntline. In 1869 he had just completed a lengthy tour of the West which had incidentally provided him with some wonderful new material. Returning from California he had stopped off in Fort McPherson, Nebraska, where he talked at length to William Frederick Cody, the once and future Buffalo Bill.

In the history of the West, the date of that meeting, 24 July 1869, has a far better claim to immortal significance than, say, 25 June 1876 (Custer's Last Stand) or 26 October 1881 (the gunfight at the O.K. Corral). Out of that encounter came not merely a new Western hero but an entire new image of the West, and an image ultimately created by the most successful example of showbusiness of its day. This image was ecstatically received, enshrined in memory and credited as truth and it therefore formed an indispensable element in creating fertile ground for the reception of the myth to come.

Buffalo Bill Cody has the unique distinction of first being invented by a dime novelist and then re-inventing himself. Because he had a short and successful career as an actor and a long and spectacular career as a showman, it is often assumed that, as a frontiersman, he was a fraud. He did not do much to dispel this impression by his autobiography, which is padded with tall tales and sections plagiarised from others' laudatory accounts of his exploits. He happily endorsed the publicity his agents dreamed up for his show. So strident did the publicity become and so enthusiastically did he encourage it, that his name did not have to wait for the debunking of Western legends which became a feature of the 1960s. On his claim that he bore the scars of 137 wounds from Indian fights, his wife caustically told reporters she had noticed only one. In 1897 journalists dug out William Matthewson of Wichita who claimed Cody had stolen the nickname and reputation of champion buffalo-killer from him. In the same year the *New York World* challenged his claim that he killed the Indian chief Tall Bull in 1869 and the details of his famous account of his single-handed slaying of Yellow Hand in 1876 were denied by eyewitnesses to it. He left the Union Army with the rank he entered it – private; he received his promotion to Colonel in 1887 when the Governor of Nebraska gave him the rank in the National Guard. Modern writers frequently refer to Cody as a charlatan and dismiss him as a braggart.

All this ignores some obvious facts. Before Judson ever 'discovered' him, Cody had led a life which gave him as much right to be considered a hero as Carson. Indeed, of all the men who became legends of the Wild West, few had as good a claim as Cody to their fame. His brief period as a rider for the Pony Express, itself to last only eighteen months in 1860-61, was dangerous and did involve one exceptionally long ride of 384 miles, though it was no more remarkable than the experiences of others employed in this ill-conceived enterprise. His claim that he killed a record 4,280 buffalo while under contract to supply meat to the Kansas Pacific Railroad appears to be correct; it was the construction crews (not Ned Buntline) who named him Buffalo Bill. Because trick-shot stars in shows and fairs, like Cody himself later, often cheated by replacing bullets with cartridges made up with bird-shot, it has sometimes been assumed Cody's tales of his marksmanship were just fables.* They were not. General Eugene A. Carr, his commanding officer when he was a scout for the Fifth Cavalry, wrote in his testimonial for Cody in 1878: 'I could not believe that a man could be certain to shoot antelope running till I had seen him do it so often.'

Cody's real distinction lies in his career as a scout for the Army from 1868. Even before then, a St. Louis newspaper was already calling him 'the noted guide.' His record, as his biographer Don Russell has pointed out, was impressive to say the least. He served continuously from September 1868 to November 1872 (the longest period known for any scout) and was involved in fourteen expeditions and fifteen Indian fights. The balance of the evidence suggests he did indeed kill Chief Tall Bull in 1869 (though not in hand-to-hand combat with knives, as his publicity later claimed). He was never, as he insisted he was, made chief of scouts for the Fifth Cavalry, but Carr thought so highly of him that he arranged extra pay 'for extraordinary good services.' His reputation as a scout is indicated by General Sheridan's request for him to act as guide for

---

* Use of birdshot also of course ensured that the audience was not accidentally depleted.

a hunting-party of Eastern VIPs in September 1871 and again for the Grand Duke Alexis of Russia in January 1872. When the campaign against the Sioux began in 1876, the Army specifically requested his services. Ten days after the news of the Custer massacre was known, the unit of the Third Cavalry to which Cody was attached was involved in an Indian fight, in which Cody fought, killed and scalped the Cheyenne chief Yellow Hand. It is also often forgotten that Cody was awarded the Congressional Medal of Honor for his part in an Indian fight in April 1872. His name was removed from the Honor rolls in 1917, but simply because it had finally been noticed that, as a civilian employee of the Army and not a serving soldier, he was debarred from receiving the medal. Following a petition by his grandson, Congress restored Cody's name to the rolls in 1989.

The man therefore whom Judson met in July 1869 was worth a newspaper story or two. What he got was immortality. Judson immediately sold to Street and Smith *Buffalo Bill, King of the Border Men*, a lurid tale not of the Wild West but of the Civil War in Kansas, and one which bore the sketchiest resemblance to any events in Cody's life. No matter: Street and Smith advertised it as biography:

> All the friends of Ned Buntline should read of *Buffalo Bill*, who is a living SCOUT, and after enjoying reading of the daring adventurer, the best horseman, the best informed guide, and the greatest hunter, should go among their friends and tell them what a splendid *true* story we are now publishing in the *New York Weekly*. In the words of Ned, "It is the *wildest, truest story* I ever wrote."

Judson then turned the novel into a melodrama, as a result of which Cody's life was transformed. Prompted by offers of hospitality from the prominent men for whom he had acted as a guide, Cody went East in 1872 and was greeted in Chicago and New York as a celebrity. He looked up Judson and was promptly dragged to see the play and to take a bow. Judson then pestered Cody to consider playing himself on stage. He finally agreed and together with his friend John Burwell 'Texas Jack' Omohundro, joined Judson in Chicago for all three to act in *The Scouts of the Prairie*, concocted by Judson on the spot. It is disappointing to discover that the drama critic of the *Chicago Times* on learning the play had been written in four hours did not ask (as Cody says in his autobiography): how had Judson spent the time? Atrocious as drama though it may have been, it toured six cities with great success and ended its run in New York.

Cody had found a new career. He broke with Judson at the end of the 1872 season, possibly disappointed with his share of the box-office receipts, and formed his own company, The Buffalo Bill

Combination, to play frontier melodramas. For the next nine years he alternated between making a good living as an actor during the season and then returning to the West, usually to act as a guide or scout. A report of the fight with Yellow Hand, written by J.V. Arlington, and grossly overwritten at that, appeared within days of the event in the *New York Weekly*. Cody then persuaded Arlington to write a melodrama based on the incident, so that the following season, *The Red Right Hand, or, the First Scalp for Custer* played to packed houses all over the East. In 1878 Cody teamed up with Prentiss Ingraham, Southern gentleman, dandy and dime novelist *extraordinaire*, who wrote several melodramas for the Buffalo Bill Combination and kept up a close association with Cody.

One of the most immediate fruits of this arrangement was the beginning of the extraordinary phenomenon of the Buffalo Bill dime novel. Estimates of the total number have always varied widely, but the best evidence suggests 557 originals and, including reprints and re-titled numbers, about 1,700 issues overall. Judson wrote only four and Cody probably wrote some himself. Sometime around 1880 Ingraham began ghostwriting for him and under one pseudonym or another went on to produce about 120 Buffalo Bill titles. As a figure in literature of any kind, no-one has approached then or since the popularity, measured by books published, of Buffalo Bill.*

Where Cody, aided by his press agent John Burke, showed remarkable skill was in weaving together his personae in the dime novels, on stage and in real life, so that the public was bombarded with the image of the heroic frontiersman. Cody certainly made a good living as an actor; his claim that he had made $135,000 by 1879 is probably another of his exaggerations but he was probably clearing $100 per week average. In the theatre however Cody was a fad and the fad faded, so he took the decision to retire from the stage in 1882. In 1877, with his old friend Major Frank North, he had bought a ranch in Nebraska. There in 1882 he staged a very successful Fourth of July celebration along the lines of a rodeo. The well-known impresario Nate Salisbury, looking for a variation on the circuses already attracting large audiences across the United States, persuaded Cody to consider organising a touring show with a Wild West theme. Cody made an abortive start by taking as a partner Dr. W.F. Carver, marksman, braggart and confidence man. This 'Wild West, Rocky Mountain and Prairie Exhibition' made some money on tour through the Mid-West and East but broke up at the end of the year. Cody then did what he should have done in the first place and went

---

* Curiously, Cody has been also the real-life figure most often portrayed in films.

into partnership with Salisbury. In 1883 Buffalo Bill's Wild West was born.

Buffalo Bill Cody's contribution to preparing the ground for the myth of the West is difficult to overestimate. In three distinct but interlinked areas – the theatre, the dime novel and exhibition entertainment – he did more than any other individual, or indeed any other combination of factors, to recreate the image of the Wild West in the mind of the American public. That image, not an understanding of the forces of history, nor the simple facts of the conquest of the frontier, underpinned what was to become the myth. The irony of Cody's fate was to be overtaken by the rise of the myth and to be discarded because his vision of the West was no longer in tune with the central tenets of the myth itself.

Frontier dramas in the theatre did not begin with Buffalo Bill. There is no question however that *Scouts of the Prairie* began a fashion. America's most popular playwright of the age, Bartley Campbell, turned to the West with *The Vigilantes, or, the Heart of the Sierras* in 1878. This basic morality play was not particularly well received, but in the following year *My Partner* opened in New York to sustained acclaim. Campbell had elevated the Western play but beneath that level the success of Cody's Combination encouraged a host of imitators producing simple melodramas, filled with gunfire, Indians and the triumph of the plainsman. The critics were usually unimpressed. Of *The Vigilantes* the *New York Herald* wrote that it was '...entirely devoid of the interest with which an intelligent playwright may invest both dialogue and action, *even in this department'* [italics added]. The fashion which Cody had set however rested on real public approval. Obviously, frontier melodramas were exotic and exciting. More importantly, as Rosemary K. Bank has argued, their characters became symbols: the plays showed individuals participating in the nation's destiny, they represented the chance for a fresh start and success by personal effort.

Buffalo Bill dime novels decisively gave a new direction to the image of the West in popular literature. Though old themes and old stereotypes persisted, the Buffalo Bill stories dictated a different emphasis. Cooper and his imitators had always insisted that the hero be a gentleman, usually an Easterner – the Leatherstocking figure was there to teach him how to be heroic in the West. Now the hero was a self-made man succeeding through rugged individualism. Whether set in mountains, mining camps or on the plains, this hero was the scout, the new leader of the march of civilisation, and, though he might have to clean up nasty deposits of bandits, gold thieves, Mexicans and renegades, his real job was removing Indians.

The level of violence therefore went up on an exponential scale, not least for commercial reasons – when asked how Beadle and Adams had met competition from their rivals, their editor Orville Victor laconically replied: 'We had to kill a few more Indians.'

Few of the writers had any knowledge of the West and even those who had visited the frontier, like Judson and Ingraham, had little interest in portraying it accurately. Apart from the routine slaughter which would have left not an Indian alive within a decade, the Western gunfight was given some bizarre treatment. The cover of the 1894 *Wild Bill, the Wild West Duelist* (ostensibly written by Cody) shows a dashing Hickok, back-to-back with his villainous opponent, pistols raised and cocked, waiting for the signal to pace off in the approved formal European fashion. Mark Twain's description of the arrangements for the ludicrous French duel in *Tramp Abroad* would be the perfect comment:

> I have never had any such experience of such a swell duel as this before. I have had a good deal to do with duels on the Pacific coast, but I see now they were crude affairs.

At this distance of time it is difficult to grasp the scale of the popularity and success of Buffalo Bill's Wild West show. Cody and Salisbury's management lasted until 1894, when Barnum & Bailey replaced Salisbury until the show's demise in 1909. During that time it toured the United States each year, with a major lengthy booking in New York, went to Canada in 1885 and made its first visit to Europe in 1887. Cody consistently claimed that he was presenting not a mere outdoor spectacular entertainment, but an authentic encapsulation of life in the West. It therefore had Indians directly from the reservations (Sitting Bull joined in 1885), former working cowboys, the original Deadwood stage and its own small herd of buffalo. The format of the show contained parades of Western characters and exhibitions of horsemanship and marksmanship but focussed on set-piece re-enactments of frontier 'events.' Among these were (inevitably) Cody's duel with Yellow Hand, Indian attacks on a settler's cabin, and on the Deadwood stage (both defeated by the timely arrival of the cowboys) and Custer's Last Stand (Sitting Bull was often hissed when he appeared).

An explanation of the show's success is not difficult to find. Cody was an instinctive and inspired showman, yet through his showmanship shone his almost child-like sincerity that he was bringing the reality of the West to the world. The show's publicity machine was outstandingly effective: its advance work was meticulous – giant posters were displayed, the local press mobilised and local dignitaries wooed by the principals. While on the one hand the publicity men claimed the educational value of the show, on the other they organised and timed the appearance of Buffalo Bill dime novels. The height of the show's success was its run in Chicago during the 1893 World's Fair. Thereafter it went into a slow decline. Even after it closed, Cody himself could not quit since a lifetime of carelessness with his huge profits and a series of disastrous investments had left him in deep financial trouble. He joined a rival show in 1909 and, when that went broke in 1913, he appeared in a circus and then in the last remaining major Wild West vehicle, the Miller 101 Ranch show. He made his final farewell performance (the first was in 1910!) in December 1916 and died a few weeks later.

Buffalo Bill's was not the only Wild West show; its first rival appeared within five years and by the 1890s there were fifty or more, of varying sizes, operating across the United States. Nevertheless, Cody's boast that he brought the West to the rest of America was no idle one. Even at the beginning, the audiences were large – 44,445 people saw the show in Chicago in 1884 and in 1885 one million saw it in five months' touring. From 1886 Cody had a permanent venue on Staten Island for New York and one week in July showed receipts for 193,960 attendances. The 1893 World's Fair in Chicago attracted an estimated 27 million people; six million of them took the opportunity to see the show in its grounds nearby. Anxious to dispel any notion that it was some kind of circus, Cody never permitted the use of the word 'show' after the title Buffalo Bill's Wild West. From the beginning, Cody insisted that he was bringing not the history of the West, but its present, or at worst very recent, reality. All the publicity laid great stress on the realism of what was portrayed, right down to claiming that the Indians in the show were so dangerous that the reservations had lent them to him with relief. For a decade, this illusion of authenticity convinced audiences that the show offered them not an enactment but the reality of the victorious march into the West. Mark Twain gave it his personal endorsement:

> It brought back to me the breezy, wild life of the Rocky Mountains, and stirred me like a war song. Down to its smallest details, the show is genuine – cowboys, *vaqueros*, Indians, stage coach, costumes and all...

In fact, the publicity men shaped the show around what experience taught them the public liked, and what the public liked were violence and the fights with the Indians. One long-used programme accordingly began: 'The Bullet is the Pioneer of Civilisation, for it has gone hand-in-hand with the axe that cleared the forest and with the Bible and the school book.' Cody was thus trapped into portraying the *Wild* West, but in the 1890s Americans were no longer confident of the worth of progress and they were being urged to look to the West as the source of values which civilisation seemed to have lost. Trapped in a lifetime of simple preconceptions, this was a West Cody could not display.

Well before it entered its long decline however, Buffalo Bill's Wild West had made a decisive contribution to the creation of one final image central to the myth which was about to emerge. By 1887 the definitive Western hero was no longer the plainsman, let alone the forest hunter or mountain man – it was the cowboy.

Chapter Four

The Knights of the Range

...arouse their ire, and your life is of no more value in their esteem than that of a coyote. Morally, as a class, they are foul-mouthed, blasphemous, drunken, lecherous, utterly corrupt.

Frank Leslie's Illustrated Weekly, 1 December 1883

Altogether cow-boys are a whole-souled, large-hearted, generous class of fellows... and it is safe to say that nine-tenths of the hard things that have been said of them have come from men who never knew intimately a single one of them.

Harper's Weekly, 16 October 1886

As the last of heroes to emerge from the frontier, the cowboy was unique: the only quality he shared with his distinguished predecessors was that he lived in the West. He came as no pioneer leading settlers; he found no trails and passes for others to reach new lands; he did not guide soldiers and wagon trains across the trackless prairies; and he rarely (never by choice, least of all as an avocation) fought Indians. Indeed, if nobility of purpose, expressed in some sort of social utility, is the hallmark of the Western hero hitherto, he had none of it and it had to be entirely invented for him. Moreover, all previous frontier hero-stereotypes were epitomised in great representative individuals, but the collective American memory has left the cowboy anonymous. The basic reason is simple: there *was* no great representative because there was nothing much to represent. In comparison with previous heroes, the cowboy is not partly but entirely a cultural artifact.

The economic circumstances which produced the cowboy are well known, though it is often forgotten that the United States had an important cattle industry from colonial times and therefore long before the exploitation of the Western grasslands began. Western cattle-ranching was the product of a particular set of factors – a combination of unusual economic conditions, Federal land policy and a benign period in the weather cycle. The cattle boom which mushroomed as a result collapsed after twenty years from the stupidity and greed of the cattlemen and the nemesis of the West's uncertain climate.

A version of open-range ranching had begun long before the Civil War in Texas where the stock and techniques had been acquired from the Mexicans (as the vocabulary obviously reveals). Texas cattlemen had begun long drives to Louisiana and even, briefly in the 1850s, to California, but the Civil War deprived Texas of access to any external markets and the cattle simply multiplied unchecked and in the wild. Thus in 1865 a huge supply was available for Midwestern slaughterhouses and packing plants, which were linked by a good railroad network to Eastern demand. Texas however had no such railroad linkage to the Mid-West and an attempt to drive cattle north for sale in 1866 found no profits for the scrawny, trail-weary beasts.

The building of the Kansas Pacific Railroad, begun in 1866, incidentally provided cattlemen with railheads on well-watered grass for fattening. The first of these was exploited by Joseph McCoy in 1867 at Abilene and thereafter cowtowns sprang up in succession as the railroad moved west. From the Red River country, the railheads were still 400 miles away (a thousand from the Nueces River), so the drive north took at least two to three months. Nevertheless, an estimated 6 to 9 million cattle had made the drive by 1886, when the completion of the Texas and Pacific Railroad made it unnecessary. From 1880 however an even longer drive, of five to six months, had been bringing herds up from Texas to the relatively empty grasslands of the Northwest – to Nebraska, eastern Colorado, Wyoming, Montana and Dakota.

This expansion of the industry rested simply on the advantages of the open range. Unlike the East and Mid-West, where land was owned and cattle were pastured, watered and sheltered, in the West cattle grazed on the public domain and fended entirely for themselves: the overheads were thus minimal. By 1880 it was being commonly said that a $5 Texas calf could be sold as a steer for $35 to $45 in Chicago and that, allowing for all overheads, profits of 25% to 40% after five years were virtually guaranteed. Inevitably a boom resulted, fuelled by vigorous promotion from railroads looking for business and irresponsible writers like James S. Brisbin, whose *The Beef Bonanza, or, How to Get Rich on the Plains*, like most of this literature, played down the real costs. Nevertheless, capital flooded in from corporations in the East and abroad, notably Britain, and vast herds were built up from Texas to Montana. Most of the cattle companies quickly found the costs were higher and the profits lower than they had anticipated, but even so the largest of them all, the Scots-owned Prairie Cattle Company, with ranges from Texas to Colorado, was paying a dividend of 20·5% in 1883.

The bubble burst in the mid-1880s. Cattle sales glutted the market, so that the price fell from $35 per head in 1882 to $8 in 1885. The ranges had become overstocked – ranchers assumed 15 to 30 acres, depending on grass quality, to feed a cow but had still foolishly pressed resources beyond their limits. The weather however was the killer. A severe drought in Texas in 1884 was followed by a dreadful winter in the Southwest in 1885-86 and the winter of 1886-87 in the Northwest was the worst ever recorded. It is difficult to estimate average losses, but it is likely that Montana and Wyoming saw at least 35% of the cattle dead and in some areas the figure reached 90%.

Traditional open range ranching never recovered from this disaster. What emerged after 1887 was a version of efficient corporate enterprise. Practices already introduced by the more prudent cattle companies now became standard. Smaller herds of quality stock replaced Texas longhorns and were grazed on land more and more likely to be fenced; prime pasture and water-access were controlled and costs ruthlessly watched and pared. These developments, together with the spread of railroad links, ended for ever the round-up and long drive and with their disappearance the cowboy in essence became just another kind of farmhand.

Even for their heyday, hard data about cowboys are difficult to find. No certain figure can be given for their total number: George W. Saunders, founder in 1915 of the Texas Trail Drivers (a cowboy alumni association) wrote: 'It is estimated that 35,000 men went up the trails with the herds' but he does not say who did the estimating. Philip Ashton Rollins, ex-cowboy and cattleman and writer, judged that most white cowboys were Southerners, with the addition of some Midwesterners and foreigners. Saunders firmly stated that one third were black and Mexican, a figure which William Savage finds statistically unlikely; Philip Durham and Everett Jones estimate one-seventh were black, while Jack Weston suggests 20% black and 10% Mexican. Few authorities offer much detail on the role of native Americans, but a handful of contemporaries were prepared to admit, in retrospect, that the best cowboys were probably Indians.

Better information exists on cowboys' work and its rewards. Cowboys worked the season, at the end of which most were laid off, for fewer than 20% were kept on to work through the year. They moved from employer to employer, were young (the open-range era embraced one generation and the work was too onerous for the middle-aged) and single, for employers offered no facilities for married men. The work was by every account exceptionally hard and often dangerous – Texans insisted that, though they had learned much from Mexicans, open-range ranching required unique skills because the cattle were essentially wild beasts and herded in wild country. It is often said that cowboys were badly paid; this is a statement requiring some qualification. Weston has shown that a cowboy earning an average of $300 per annum made twice as much as a farm worker and a good deal more than most industrial workers, given that the cowboy's food, fuel and ranch accommodation were free. If however cowboys' insistence that they possessed and deployed exceptional skills is believed, then their wages were one quarter of those of the small aristocracy of skilled industrial workers who earned $1200 a year or more. When owners cut wages in the 1880s, as part of the effort to reduce costs, there were several cowboy strikes and some joined the labour union organisation of the Knights of Labor.

In surveying the life and work of the cowboy and the cattle industry which created him, virtually everyone who has written seriously about the West admits there is precious little to justify legendary status, let alone the cowboy's position at the core of what was to become the myth. This glorious future in myth is even more peculiar when it has to be recognised that for two-thirds of their short existence, cowboys were seen not as heroes at all, but villains. What is particularly intriguing is the way the image of the cowboy in the public mind switched from ruffian to hero and the speed with which this happened. Without this transformation the myth-makers at the century's end would have been lost for their essential material.

Until the mid-1880s cowboys were not only not admired, they were viewed with fear and abhorrence: newspaper reports indicate they were drunken delinquents at best and violent criminals at worst. The evidence for the existence of this widespread view is overwhelming. Those who had direct contact with cowboys stressed it – an Ellsworth, Kansas, paper noted in 1873 that 'The Lipan and the Comanche are not more unlike the civilized white man than is the nomadic herdsman to the Texan who dwells in the city or cultivates the plains.' Joseph McCoy, who of course knew the cowboy at first hand, wrote in 1874 that, once payed off, a cowboy plunged into a 'vortex of dissipation,' so that soon 'anger and bad whiskey urge him on to deeds of blood and death' and at such times it 'was not safe to

be on the streets, or for that matter within a house, for a drunk
cowboy would as soon shoot into a house as at anything else.'
Richard I. Dodge, former aide to General Sherman, wrote in 1882
that the cowboy '...is the most reckless of all the reckless desperadoes
developed on the frontier...his visits to the frontier towns of Kansas
and Nebraska being regarded as a calamity second only to a Western
tornado.'

This attitude was quickly picked up by Eastern papers and
therefore fixed in the public mind. The rival New York popular
weeklies, *Frank Leslie's Illustrated Weekly* and the *Police Gazette*
were vying for circulation with sensational stories and copious
woodcut illustrations and seized on cowboys as a stock source of
lurid copy. Lonn Taylor has written that virtually every issue of
these two papers in the late 1870s and early 1880s carried at least
one illustration of cowboys in lawless and violent behaviour. This
is something of an exaggeration. The first mention of cowboys by
name in the *Police Gazette* is in the issue for 10 August 1878, which
ran an item from Dodge City mentioning Wyatt Earp having trouble with some Texas 'cow-boys;' the use of the inverted commas
suggests the term is new to readers. Though accounts of crime in
the West figure large, there is only one specific reference to cowboys
in 1879, in a piece for 6 September entitled 'The Cow-Boy of the
Plains. A Sketch of a Very Boisterous and Often Murderous Character.' After four column inches describing the work and dress of
the cowboy, there are two paragraphs of pious horror at his behaviour in the cowtowns:

> While in town his home is in the saloons and the dance houses. He soon
> gets gloriously drunk and then begins to yell like a wild Indian and
> shoots off his big revolvers promiscuously into the crowd. He is little
> else than a crazy demon at such times and woe betide the man who
> crosses his path.

Pieces of this kind then appeared with increasing frequency and
of marked similarity. *Frank Leslie's* for 14 January 1881 gave some
space to cowboy skills and then added a new crime – wholesale
robbery:

> When "off-duty" cowboys are a terror in the way they manifest their
> exuberance of spirits. Two or three will dash through a town, and, before
> the people know what is going on, will have robbed every store of
> importance and made their escape.

This short article was accompanied by a dramatic illustration
entitled 'A Common Incident in Southwestern Life. The Capture of

a Texas Town by Cowboys.' In December the following year the
paper modified its line slightly:

> You are as safe with them alone on the plains as with any class of men,
> so long as you do not impose upon them...But impose upon them, or
> arouse their ire, and your life is of no more esteem than that of a coyote.
> Morally, as a class, they are foul-mouthed, blasphemous, drunken,
> lecherous, utterly corrupt...This dark picture of the cowboys ought,
> however to be lightened by the statement that there is occasionally a
> white sheep among the black...

The quality periodicals also ran items in the same vein. *Scribner's*
magazine for March 1880 ran a seven-and-a-half page article titled
'Over Sunday in New Sharon' (a pseudonym for Dodge City). The
style is more elevated than *Frank Leslie's* or the *Police Gazette*, but
the sentiments are the same:

> ...the herder or "cow-boy" dominates the town. He is no longer the
> easy-going, mild-demeanored type of native Texan languor and the
> anomalous self-repression of the trail; he "turns loose," as he calls it,
> and appears to change his disposition in the act of shifting his garments,
> so rapidly does he challenge every restraint of society, and sound every
> depth of vice and shame...he becomes a spendthrift, a drunkard, a
> gambler, a libertine, and too often, alas, a murderer!

By 1885 this image had begun a dramatic transformation. The
popular weeklies were now printing more and more pieces indicating
the cowboy was just another figure who proved how amusingly crude
and unsophisticated the West was. This line had of course been
commonplace for fifty years for successive frontiers. It had received
a stylish filip from Mark Twain, notably in his immensely entertain-
ing account of his trip across the plains and time in Nevada described
in *Roughing It*, published in 1872. The new trend in the weeklies
differed from the old only in owing something (though not enough)
to Twain's humour. The really decisive shift occurred in the up-
market magazines. In October 1886 *Harper's Weekly* began an item
entitled 'Some Facts About Cowboys:'

> Cow-boys as a class are brimful and running over with wit, merriment,
> good-humour. They are always ready for a bit of innocent fun, but are
> not perpetually spoiling for a fight, as has so often been said of them.

These jolly fellows naturally could not be blamed for playing a
few pranks at the expense of eastern dudes who were foolish enough
to stand on their dignity but, since a cowboy was deprived of the sort
of amusements available to young Easterners '...it is but natural that

his exuberance of spirits should cause him to find sport of other
kinds' – no longer, it seems, by robbing all the stores in town. It was
admitted that:

> They have been known...to resort to acts of real abuse and injury
> against defenceless people. But such acts on the part of genuine cowboys
> are rare, and are rigorously condemned by all the respectable element
> in the business.

In a fine gesture toward previous comment, the writer went on:

> Altogether cow-boys are a whole-souled, large-hearted, generous class
> of fellows...and it is safe to say that nine-tenths of the hard things that
> have been said of them have come from men who never knew a single
> one of them.

So much for Joseph McCoy and Richard Dodge! This article was
accompanied by a large illustration, by Rufus Zogbaum, of a group
of cowboys galloping through a western town brandishing their
revolvers – but the effect is not the violence and villainy of the *Frank
Leslie's* woodcuts of five years before; these cowboys are young,
dashing, and *romantic*.

In 1884 the New York weeklies did not admit there was a respectable element in the cowboy 'business:' in 1886 cowboys were given
their first coating of social utility. In November, *Harper's New
Monthly Magazine* published an article by Joseph Nimmo, head of
the Bureau of Statistics, who the previous year had published a major
report on the cattle industry. Nimmo referred in passing to the
cowboy's 'generous and *heroic* [italics added] traits of character' and
then argued that 20,000 cowboys* had been 'a corps of mounted
scouts' who have pacified the frontier so that 'an unarmed man may
now travel alone throughout Wyoming, Dakota, Montana and
Idaho, and even in Texas as safely as in the New England or the
Middle States.' Cowboys, noble fellows, had helpfully, given the
weakness of the overstretched Army, put an end to the Indian
menace.

Within a two-year period the volte-face of the Eastern press
marked the transformation of the cowboy's image. It was signalled
by the publication in 1885 of the first cowboy autobiography,
Charles A. Siringo's *A Texas Cowboy, or, Fifteen Years on the
Hurricane Deck of a Spanish Pony*. Siringo was born in 1856 and had
begun working as a cowboy in his early 'teens; in later life he became
a range detective and worked for the Pinkerton agency but in 1885

---

*Should this be accepted as a base figure rather than G.W. Saunders's 35,000?

was trying his hand as a small trader in Caldwell, Kansas. The preface to *A Texas Cowboy* explains why Siringo wrote it: '...money, and lots of it.' The subtitle is easy to comprehend – it is an obvious joking reference to the great popularity of the dime novel sea story. What needs explanation is Siringo's belief, in 1885, that a cowboy's life story would sell. Siringo himself gives no hint, merely making the conventional excuse that it is best for a tyro author to write about what he knows. J. Frank Dobie speculated that Siringo was stimulated by reading in the Caldwell newspaper items on cowboys reprinted from the Eastern press, indicating a widespread interest. It is difficult to judge exactly how well *A Texas Cowboy* did sell. In 1919 Siringo claimed a million copies, which can be dismissed as another Western tall tale. The book was published first in Caldwell, then in Chicago in 1886 and then, significantly, in a paperback edition by Rand, McNally sometime before one of their subsidiaries produced a hardback edition in 1893. Taken together these must have produced many thousands of copies before the known figure of 156,000 for the years 1901 to 1926. Was Siringo a cause or an effect of the revolution in attitude to the cowboy? He may have been both, by cashing in on the beginnings of a trend and then helping accelerate it, but his popularity from the 1890s on seems pretty certainly the result of the growth of the myth.

Don Russell has written: 'Just how the cowboy reputation became completely reversed within a couple of decades cannot be explained completely, for no one can forecast or analyse the popularity of an idea.' This is a touch pessimistic. Analysing the evidence shows that the switch took a couple of years, not a couple of decades and the factors which explain it, though complex, are not impenetrable. First of all, the image of the cowboy as a lawless ruffian was part of a much wider Eastern view which saw the whole West as crude and violent. Its crudity was mocked in the classic tradition of sneering at the frontier settlements. The *Police Gazette* ran items in 1878-79, for example, on tottering elderly Westerners boasting about what fearsome fighters they were, on a faro player winning $28,000 playing in his sleep, a judge hurling an impudent attorney bodily out of his court, a Nevada dance 'typically' ending in a riot and the spectacular Saturday night boozing in Virginia City.

The picture of the West as inhabited largely by desperadoes was fed from two sources, one fact, the other fiction. The Eastern weeklies drew on correspondents from all over the United States who supplied items from the local papers. Statistically, crime from the East and Mid-West far outweighed reports of nefarious activities in the West. But Western crime, like its milieu, was exotic – stagecoach robberies in Wyoming, Colorado and Dakota, horse-theft in the cattle country, mayhem in the mining camps of Nevada, Colorado and Dakota and lynchings everywhere, usually patronisingly justified on the grounds that local law enforcement was weak and so summary justice was better than none. To the East, the West *was* alarmingly lawless.

Dime novels had taken all this as subject-matter since the 1870s and produced heroes suitable to the background. The most famous of these was Edward Lytton Wheeler's creation, Deadwood Dick, who first sprang into action in 1877 and fought his way through 31 stories until the death of his creator in 1885, at which point Beadle and Adams introduced Deadwood Dick Jr., indistinguishable from his sire and hero of a further 97 novels. Deadwood Dick was a plainsman whose main role seemed to be sorting out wickedness in the mining camps, but stage robbers, kidnappers and Calamity Jane absorbed any spare time. As a hero, Deadwood Dick was virile, violent and invincible in combat but not as invariably pure in thought and deed as Buffalo Bill – given to moods of rage and despair he might on occasion operate outside the law. Street and Smith naturally produced a rival – Diamond Dick, first created by William W. Cook, alias W.B. Lawson, and continued by writers like Samuel S. Hall; another imitation appeared with Leon Lewis's Daredeath Dick. These figures were not entirely creatures of fantasy. It is possible Wheeler based Deadwood Dick on Richard W. Clarke, miner, bandit, cavalry trooper, Pony Express rider and Army scout, while Cook/Lawson may have used Richard Tanner, scout for Custer and later a trick-shot in a Wild West show. Apart from the various Dicks, the bulk of all dime fiction on the West up to 1900 concentrated on its wildness and peopled it with desperadoes.

It is unsurprising therefore that the cowboy, as a new frontier type, should have been presented as another violent and lawless element from the savage land. There was moreover a further reason: most of the early cowboys were Texans and Texas was perceived as a particularly violent state. This was in part due to the influence of, again, the widely-read *Police Gazette*. Richard Kyle Fox, the *Gazette's* editor, was a newspaperman of extraordinary ability and intuitive judgment. He had turned the *Gazette* into an immensely popular weekly in the East, with a nationwide circulation through subscription, on a formula of sensational reporting of crime and human interest stories and dramatic illustrations. He was also a man of deep prejudices, for which the *Gazette* was a vehicle. Some were admirable, for Fox detested pretension, humbug, hypocrisy and injustice. This could lead to some notable crusades in good causes –

but when translated into specific targets, Fox's solemn rages and vindictive sarcasm tended to be directed indiscriminately at the rich, most foreigners but especially the British, racial minorities, clergymen in general and Quakers in particular. In October 1878 the wrath of Fox fell on Texas.

Presumably Fox must have noted, in the weekly catalogue of the nation's crime, that Texas reports not only figured largely but that they mostly referred to killings. An item in September commented '...the people of Texas are disgusted with the evident bribery of their courts, which habitually acquit the most habitual of assassins...' But a month later the editorial decided it was not the judicial system but Texans themselves who were to blame:

> There are at the loosest calculation an average of fifteen or twenty people – most men but occasionally women – murdered every week in the state of Texas...The fact is, the murderer is a hero with the people, the press and the clergy of Texas.

It was certainly the case that of all the crimes reported in the *Gazette* for 1878 relating to the West, Texas accounted for one third. In 1879 they were up to 40% and Fox launched a crusade. Typical headlines read: 'Terrible Texans,' 'Bold Bad Bill Barb – Record of Another Typical Texas Murder Fiend,' 'Another Murder Horror from the Homicidal State,' and 'The Texas Murder Bulletin.' The crusade was given point by a genuine outrage. In April the well-known Eastern actor Benjamin Porter was shot dead and his companion Maurice Barrymore* wounded by a local gunman, James Currie, in Marshall, Texas. Both men were unarmed and protecting an actress whom Currie was pestering. The case became a *cause célèbre* in the East and focussed a good deal of hostility against Texas, and in this furore the *Gazette* took the lead.** Throughout the late 1870s and early 1880s, Texan violence and apparent contempt for law was an image from time to time maintained in the national press generally.

Texas's reputation was not entirely unjustified, for peculiar historical conditions caused the persistence of a chronic high level of violence, particularly in the central region, for most of the second half of the nineteenth century. During the Civil War, anti-abolition-

---

* The father of Ethel, John and Lionel Barrymore.
** The Eastern chorus of condemnation predictably aroused Texan patriotism, though Western papers divided over the case. Currie had claimed from the start that with his local 'connections' and a sympathetic jury he had nothing to fear; in the event he proved to be absolutely correct and walked scot free, for at his trial in June 1880 he was found not guilty by reason of insanity!

ist hysteria culminated in the lynching of 42 suspected Union sym-
pathisers at Gainesville in 1862. Vendettas between Confederate
loyalists and marauding gangs, like the notorious Heel Flies, ostensibly supporting the North-imposed state government, marred the
Reconstruction era. Between 1870 and 1875 a serious threat was
posed by the revival of Comanche and Kiowa raids; though sup-
pressed after the revival of the Frontier Brigade of the Texas Rangers
in 1874, the danger had left a permanently armed citizenry and a kind
of 'war psychology.' Post-Civil War instability showed itself also in
concentrations of horse and cattle thieves, who were met with persistent vigilante action. In 1878 Kimble County was such a nest of
thieves that it proved impossible to find sufficient 'honest' men to
form a vigilance group, so the Rangers were obliged to take over. In
general, vigilantism remained endemic until the 1890s. The activities
of emergent cattle barons produced serious conflict, exemplified in
the career of Isom Prentiss Olive, who from 1869 fought a guerrilla
war with his smaller neighbours.* In the 1880s and through the
1890s, cattlemen fencing off the range provoked armed conflict, in
1883-84 widespread enough to be called the Fence Cutters' War.
Both a cause and a result of this endemic violence was a Texan
tradition of the right of self-defence and self-redress, without re-
course to law, unique in the United States.

Up to the early 1880s then, so long as cowboys were associated
with Texas they would carry a stigma. The development of the ranges
of the Northwest was to change that view considerably. The first to
point out that the cowboys of Wyoming and Montana were a very
different breed from their Texas counterparts were not Americans at
all, but British visitors. As early as 1880, William Baillie-Grohman,
a Scot who had hunted and travelled extensively in the West, wrote
'There are a good many false notions abroad respecting the general
character of Western man...stockmen...as a rule, I found to be a
thrifty, energetic and very hospitable class.' The West may, he went
on, be '...inhabited in our fancy by a race of desperadoes, whose only
law is the revolver, whose only god is whisky, and whose one prayer
is foul-mouthed blasphemy. This however is not so...' Wistfully, he
did warn however that '...the English settler will for some time sadly
miss the social laws which govern the intercourse of different classes
in the Old World.' Four years later James S. Tait, of the Scots cattle

---

* 'Print' Olive and his outfit re-located in Nebraska in 1876, where they provoked
another range war with the local farmers. The events followed the plot of *Shane* with
remarkable fidelity, save that more farmers were (barbarously) killed and that Olive
served a brief jail sentence after being brought to trial. Needless to say, the *Police
Gazette* targeted Olive as a Texan – and referred to his 'satellites' as cowboys.

and land brokers Tait, Denman and Co., wrote *The Cattlefields of the Far West: Their Present and Future,* in which he chose to quote a journalist fellow-countryman:

> The stories one hears about the wild cowboy and his freaks are mostly mythical; cowboys do go on a spree and run amuck once in a while, but not in the settled parts, and, generally speaking, they are a very harmless part of the community. Drunkenness is very rare – at least to me it seemed so, and I watched for it curiously.

These interesting early improvements in the cowboy's image had little impact in the United States – Baillie-Grohman wrote for the serious London magazine the *Fortnightly Review* and Tait's work was aimed at the British investor. In 1886 however Joseph Nimmo's piece for *Harper's New Monthly Magazine* did a great deal more than praise cowboys for their noble services. Nimmo explicity drew a distinction between Texas and the Northwestern ranges. Texans, he wrote, had been conditioned by Indian warfare, so their tendency to violence was at least understandable. Rustling and horse-thievery had indeed encouraged a period of lynch law in the Northwest, but now all this sort of thing was happily in the past, with important results:

> The cow-boy of today, especially on the northern ranges, is of entirely different type from the original cowboy of Texas...Organisation, discipline and order characterize the new undertakings on the northern ranges...a new class of cowboys has been introduced and developed. Some have come from Texas, and have brought with them a knowledge of the arts of their calling, but a number from the other States and Territories constitutes a large majority of the whole.

The key factor explaining this transformation, wrote Nimmo, was the participation of Eastern and foreign capital in ranching. The foreigners in particular had raised the whole tone of the business:

> Among them are also many Englishmen, Scotchmen, Frenchmen and Germans of large means, embracing titled men who have embarked in the business quite extensively...Some of this class have, from the force of romantic temperament and the exhilaration of range life, themselves participated actively in the duties of the cowboy.

The notion that the presence of foreigners, particularly the British, had dramatically changed the cowboy's character is regrettably not sustainable but the influence of the foreigners on the range should not be ignored, for it did help change the image. Wyoming was littered with the scions of the British aristocracy managing ranches: Algernon Winn, the second son of Lord St. Oswald ran the Big Horn Cattle Company, Horace Plunkett, third son of Lord Dunsany ran a spread on the Powder River, Edward Boughton, son of a baronet, managed the Ione Cattle Company on the Laramie Plains. In Colorado, Lyulph Ogilvy, younger son of the earl of Airlie, was a large cattleman. Pioneer of this British invasion was Moreton Frewen, son of an untitled Sussex gentleman, who later married Clara Jerome, sister of Jennie, the mother of Winston Churchill. In Dakota the heir to the duke of Vallambrosa attempted a major ranching and meat-packing enterprise, the baron de Mandat-Grancy operated ranches in Dakota and Nebraska and Walter, baron von Richthofen, (uncle of the future Red Baron of World War I) ran a dairy-farm in Colorado. Their impact varied a good deal. Relations with neighbours were sometimes difficult and the local press might alternate between aggressive egalitarianism and obsessive interest. A lot depended on how the foreigners behaved: some, like Frewen and Ogilvy, were popular with their cowboys, but de Mandat-Grancy, for example, was generally despised because he was too stand-offish.

Two things are clear. First, the presence of foreign ranch owners and managers gave a new air of respectability to the cattle business. Second, in addition to Southerners and Midwesterners, cowboys themselves now included Easterners and Europeans who had chosen to spend a season or so on the range. Von Richthofen, in a promotional work written in 1885, noted that: 'Among cowboys are to be found the sons of the best families, who enjoy this romantic, healthy and free life on the prairie.' The most striking testimony came from a former cowboy, W.S. James, who in 1898 followed Siringo's example and published an autobiography of his days in Texas. He recalled a camp-fire discussion which turned to education:

> Out of nine young men, the oldest in the squad being twenty-eight, it was ascertained by taking stock that five out of the nine had graduated in Eastern colleges, two of the five being U.V. [University of Virginia] graduates.

Some evidence suggests therefore that by the mid-1880s cowboys had changed a good deal from their original Texas prototype and indeed that savage Texans were now leavened with educated outsiders. Nimmo's breathless admiration however makes too much of a good thing: no leopard changes all his spots. Another British observer, John Baumann, admired cowboys but was not blind to the persistence of all the old faults. Writing for *Lippencott's Magazine* in 1886 he remarked 'Our cowboy is shockingly cruel, hasty in temper and unbridled in tongue...his contempt for life often leads to need-less bloodshed.' The following year, writing for his compatriots in the *Fortnightly Review*, he could have been paraphrasing the New York popular weeklies at the beginning of the decade. Once in a town, he wrote

> ...dissipation, gambling and riotous living soon empty their pockets, they become desperate and drunken, they quarrel with the professional gamblers and in the end the population of Boot Hill is increased.

More is needed to explain a radical shift in public attitude to cowboys than favourable pieces in Eastern papers and a new aura of semi-respectability. Several historians have agreed, more or less willingly, that once again Buffalo Bill Cody has to shoulder the blame. The evidence for Cody's role in remaking the cowboy is in fact so considerable that it is not necessary to give him more than his due. It is of course true that in his first appearances in the theatre he had as a partner his friend Texas Jack Omohundro, who was indeed a cowboy and had, as his own act, 'Texas Jack and His Lasso.' But Omohundro was a friend of Cody's because they had acted as guides for a Western hunting party together, in the theatre he played a scout, not a cowboy, and the public saw him as another scout – buckskins, slouch hat and rifle, never mind the lasso. Even when Judson quickly produced a dime novel with Jack as the hero, he was still a sort of generalised plainsman. The new, untarnished cowboy did not emerge in the theatre in 1872, but eleven years later from the Wild West show.

When William Cody went into the partnership with Major North in 1877 he clearly knew very little about cattle-ranching, or indeed about cowboys, for his autobiography suggests their skills were new to him. In no time however Cody decided that this was not the game for him:

> As there is nothing but hard work in these round-ups, having to be in the saddle all day, and standing guard over the cattle at night, rain or shine, I could not possibly find out where the fun came in...

Nevertheless, he much admired cowboys in action:

> In this cattle business is exhibited some most magnificent horsemanship, for the "cow-boys," as they are called, are invariably skillful and fearless horsemen – in fact only a most expert rider could be a cow-boy...

It was thus an obvious move, when Cody was asked to organise the Old Glory Blow-Out for 4 July 1882 at North Platte, for him to plan a series of contests of cowboy skills. Such contests were well-known – they can be traced from as early as 1847 and one had taken place at Deer Trail, Colorado in 1869 – and they would eventually become the rodeo.

Cody's notion for a travelling show, which he may have had in mind for some time, was to offer something much more elaborate – essentially open-air theatre, not a rodeo. The show he took on the road in 1883 had a format which was never basically changed, merely improved and extended, but it certainly changed its internal emphasis. Because Cody's aim was to give a living glimpse of the Wild West, the main features of the show were the spectacles – the attacks on the settlers' cabin, on a wagon train, on the Deadwood stage. About one quarter of the show was devoted to trick shooting, by Cody himself of course, and then with others (including Annie Oakley from 1885). The majority of the troupe were cowboys – some came from the ranch owned by Cody and North – and from 1883 they had a whole section for the exhibition of their skills in roping cattle, trick-riding and bronco-busting. They also, naturally, doubled as the rescue parties led by Cody to save the settlers, the wagon train and the stage. The audience was wildly enthusiastic and it looks as if Cody was actually surprised by the reception the cowboys received, but, being a smart showman, he at once enlarged their role. The section 'Cowboy Fun' was expanded and eventually the show began with a thirty-six piece 'cowboy' band playing an overture.

Cody's first step was to pick one of the cowboys and feature him, both in the show and in its publicity. The choice fell on William Levi 'Buck' Taylor, probably because of his height, for he was six feet five. In the fifteen years Taylor remained with Buffalo Bill, he became the most famous cowboy in the world and the first cowboy hero. At the start, the show's publicity men were nevertheless conscious of the need to beat the cowboy's poor image: starring cowboys then would have been like starring Hell's Angels today – it might be interesting, but was it the kind of thing the kids should see? They therefore chose to stress what a gentle fellow Taylor was – posters captioned his picture 'Amiable as a child.'

Cody himself had an important role to play. As an actor he had been notorious for carousing, proud of his remarkable capacity for hard liquor and happy to live up to the image of the tough frontiersman. Nothing much changed with the launch of the Wild West show. Of the 1883 tour, one of the publicity men wrote: 'The performers, hard-boiled plainsmen all of them, were delighted with themselves and looked upon the venture as an excursion and an excuse for a grand bust.' By 1887 all this had disappeared. Cody cleaned up his own act and imposed some discipline on his cowboys, so that the publicity men were stressing how moral and respectable the troupe was. On the tour of Europe, particularly in Britain, Cody, lionised by the upper classes, created a sensation with his impeccable manners. Referring specifically to the cowboys, he stressed that frontiersmen were truly men for all seasons – men of action in the wilderness, gentlemen in civilised society. The British press promptly and solemnly noted that the cowboy had been much misrepresented. By the time the show was running in Chicago in 1893 it was becoming commonplace for the American press to write how respectable the members of the troupe were.*

Did Buffalo Bill's Wild West have a decisive influence on changing the image of the cowboy? The idea is endorsed from a very unlikely source: Karl Marx's daughter! In 1891 Eleanor Marx and her husband George Aveling published *The Working Class Movement in America* and devoted a chapter to the cowboy as one of the 'little known proletarians.' It began:

> To most people, until lately, the cowboy was a "bold, bad man," as reckless of the lives of others as of his own, with vague values as to morals, and especially as to the rights of property, generally full of whiskey and always handy with a revolver. If the spectators of the "shows" in which he has been exhibited on both sides of the Atlantic have modified their ideas on this human subject, the modification has been, as a rule, in the direction of recognition of the fact that he is not much worse or better morally than his more civilised fellows, and in his manners, as in his physique, he is for the most part considerably the superior of these.

Distressing as it may be, particularly to those who see the cowboy as one of the symbols of American conservatism, to accept confirmation from such a source, the Marxists were right. The show projected a new image and the image reached enormous numbers of people. It is necessary to remember that its annual Staten Island venue seated 35,000 for performances twice a day and that at Chicago in 1893 audiences exceeded six million in seven months. Needless to say, Cody's fifty or so imitators featured cowboy stars in much the same mould and the travelling circuses began to include cowboy acts.

The real test of a frontier hero was not what he did in the Wild West but whether he established himself in the popular novel. Attempts have been made to find prototype cowboys in early novels.

---

* The publicity men were never given to understatement. Show hand-outs explained the performers, including the Indians, were not available to the public on Sundays because they were too busy at their prayers.

A batch of stories written between 1845 and 1848 were set on the Texas-Mexico border and produced Texas heroes, but none of these have protagonists who are discernibly cowboys. Nor do the handful of tales produced in the early 1870s by dime novelists like Joseph E. Badger, whose heroes Hurricane Bill, Mustang Sam, Pacific Pete and Panther Paul are all really Carson/Buffalo Bill plainsmen-scouts. Badger started writing about the cattle country as early as 1884, but his stories, despite the background, have no-one who can be described as a cowboy *hero*. Other dime novelists showed the same tendency. Samuel S. Hall, despite – or perhaps because of – his Western background, never wrote a story centred on cowboys as such, though of course they appear in those of the the Diamond Dick tales he wrote, and in those set in that location of his inspired invention, Sardine Box City, Arizona. Warren French has shown that one writer resolutely hostile to cowboys was Frederick Whittaker. He despised the West as barbarous, admired refined Easterners and foreigners and showed the cowboy as uncouth, violent and depraved. French did not draw the obvious link that Whittaker was merely parading the violent ruffian of *Frank Leslie's* and the *Police Gazette* articles and was thus right in tune with prevalent Eastern perceptions.

It was Cody's publicity men who took the cowboy into dime fiction. Prentiss Ingraham had been involved in Cody's publicity from his days in the theatre and had done advance work for the Wild West show, including of course manufacturing Buffalo Bill stories on a literary conveyor-belt. It was a short and obvious step to add to the marketing of Buffalo Bill the marketing of the show's new star, Buck Taylor, though there was no attempt to match the scale of the Buffalo Bill stories. The first novel featuring Taylor came in 1887 and it made the usual pretence of being biography: *Buck Taylor, King of the Cowboys, or, the Raiders and the Rangers: a Story of the Wild and Thrilling Life of William L. Taylor*. Ingraham wrote four more, all in 1891, the last being *Buck Taylor's Boys, or, the Red Riders of the Rio Grande* and then abandoned Taylor. By that time however the cowboy had been taken up by plenty of other writers.

Albert Aiken, searching for a new kind of hero to transplant to the East for a city-based plot, anticipated Clint Eastwood in *Coogan's Bluff* by eighty-six years with *Cool Colorado in New York, or, the Cowboy's Fight for a Million*. He then produced several stories centred on Dick Talbot 'the Ranch King' and 'Cowboy Deadshot' in 1892-93, by which time Leon Lewis had introduced his rival to Deadwood Dick, *Daredeath Dick, King of the Cowboys* (1890). Warren French credits William S. Patten with creating the truly noble cowboy, finally personified in Cowboy Chris, who made his debut in 1897. Patten had already introduced the clean-living ('I hope you won't think me uncivil, but I don't touch ther stuff') and freedom-loving ('Fact is, if I war rollin' in wealth, I never cu'd give up the range') cowboy in *Hustler Harry, the Cowboy Sport* in 1889 and *Wild Vulcan, the Lone Range-Rider* in 1890.

By 1887 the image of the cowboy in the public mind had been transformed from one of the more alarming manifestations of the savage land, indistinguishable from the road-agents, claim-jumpers and assorted desperadoes who were thought largely to inhabit the frontier beyond the settlements. He had become first a figure to admire and then progressed to being a hero who replaced the scout as the true representative of the frontier. But the agencies of this miraculous change could not sustain it. If the first of them was Cody's Wild West, Cody's decline affected the image of his stars. When he went into partnership with Barnum and Bailey in 1894, inevitably the show became more of an entertainment and less of Cody's vision of an intimate glimpse of the authentic West. As the 1890s wore on, the impact of all the Wild West shows diminished

The cowboy as a dime novel hero had a very short life. It is often said that the cowboy was replaced by the detective, but this is to place far too much importance on the arrival of Nick Carter in 1891 – Old Sleuth was tracking clues from 1885 and all kinds of detective fiction were popular from the late 1870s. Indeed, detectives were introduced into the West early and were so common by the 1880s it is surprising crime continued to flourish. Albert Aiken wrote *The California Detective* in 1878 and sent his creation Joe Phoenix, the Police Spy, out to the frontier several times, while Joseph Badger wrote at least three detective stories set in the West. Edward L. Wheeler not only had Deadwood Dick act as a detective in over half the tales, he also produced in 1882 the first of several stories featuring Denver Dol, the Detective Queen. St. George Rathbone took an inevitable step in 1886 when he offered up *Sombrero Sam, the Cowboy Detective*.

The trouble with the cowboy as a dime novel hero was he could not escape the straightjacket of the authors' limited imagination – he was found no distinctive plot-line that derived specifically from his role as a cowboy and he did nothing that only a cowboy could do. Dime novel cowboys fight Indians and rescue maidens from them, they fight Mexicans and bandits (who may well be the same thing), they capture kidnappers (and rescue maidens from them), they expose disguised villains and thwart their skullduggery. But these things had all been done, with just as much excitement, by scout and plainsman, by Kit Carson and Buffalo Bill, and Deadwood Dick for that matter. In fact, a lot of them had been done by Leatherstocking, which has moved several writers to insist, from Henry Nash Smith onward, that Western fiction began and ended with James Fenimore Cooper.

In cowboy dime fiction, the range is occasionally background, and sometimes well drawn, as in Joseph Badger's stories, but it is usually pretty well irrelevant to the plot-line – whatever dime novel cowboys do, herding cows is not a major part of it. Prentiss Ingraham merely used up plots from his costume drama novels of earlier years, which had the interesting result of giving cowboys the qualities and ethical code of the knight-errant – an idea which was eventually to have a great future. But not by the end of the 1890s, when the publishers were seeking fresh ideas with some desperation to hang on to their readership. Beadle and Adams went out of business in 1898, but Street and Smith forged ahead into the twentieth century with two best-selling series. One featured the clean-cut, schoolboy athlete, Frank Merriwell; the other, Jesse James.

By the mid-1890s the cowboy was on the edge of drifting into obscurity. Instead, he achieved immortality within a decade and became the final version of the hero from the frontier. This fate, which in retrospect it is easy to see was inescapable, overtook him because he became the focus of all the ideas which were coalescing into the definitive myth of the West.

Chapter Five

The Myth-Makers

...we who have felt the charm of this life, and have existed in its abounding vigor and its bold, restless freedom, will not only regret its passing for our own sakes, but must also feel real sorrow that those who come after us are not to see, as we have seen, what is perhaps the pleasantest, healthiest and most exciting phase of American existence.

> T. Roosevelt, *Ranch Life and the Hunting Trail*, 1888.

I am as you know working on a big picture book – of the West and I want you to write a preface ...telling the d—— public that this is the real old thing – step up and buy a copy – last chance – ain't going to be any more West etc.

> Frederic Remington to Owen Wister, April 1900.

The Virginian's pistol came out, and his hand lay on the table, holding it unaimed...'When you call me that, *smile!*'

> Owen Wister, *The Virginian*, 1902.

The myth of the West emerged, just as the old century ended, out of a groundswell of nationwide nostalgia. This hankering after the good old days was one response to a present that seemed to have gone very badly wrong and it took the form of an obsessive brooding about the loss of a world where special American values had flourished. There was no over-riding reason why this psychic malaise should have picked on a specific time and place. Yet within one short decade, the generalised nostalgia for a lost world was focussed on the West – and on one, particular West: the last, most recent frontier of the cattle kingdom and the cowboy. This became *the* lost world, epitomising all that America had held most precious. To a significant extent, these forces of nostalgia at work in society were focussed on the last frontier by three individuals, a politician, a painter and a writer, each of whom deliberately set out to market a personal and manufactured vision. These men, Theodore Roosevelt, Frederic Remington and Owen Wister, were the most important of the Easterners who invented the West. Since their role in popularising the West can scarcely be ignored, most historians have pointed to their importance as romantics celebrating a disappearing way of life and establishing a vivid set of images of it. What needs to be stressed is that each was a deliberate and self-conscious myth-maker.

The 1890s certainly produced serious problems, most of which were the result of forty years of rapid, transformative change. Uncontrolled economic expansion had raised the net national product by 500%, (a rate twice that of Britain at a time when Britain called herself the workshop of the world). But a price had to be paid for this expansion. Virtually unfettered by effective legal regulation, 'big business' appeared intent on erecting cartels to monopolise the market and exploit the public. Farmers felt they were the victims of business exploitation just at a time when spiralling costs and falling prices for their products left them particularly vulnerable. Growth had created wealth but not general prosperity: wealth had become polarised, so that an aristocracy of money had emerged at one extreme and a real proletariat was visible at the other. Bitter and often violent conflict between labour and employers was a regular occurrence. Moreover, between 1880 and 1910 the population had risen from 50.2 million to 92.2 million, 17.5 million of the increase coming from unrestricted immigration. A shift in the source of immigration from traditional northwest European areas to southern and eastern Europe raised fears that these newcomers, so different from the native stock, might prove unassimilable. These problems grew unchecked because the political system was judged inefficient, unresponsive and corrupt.

The end-of-century crisis was in reality a matter of facing up to the implications of what an uncritical commitment to 'progress' had produced. Faced with all this, a section of the intellectuals went into a panic and a significant proportion of the middle class followed them into tirades of abuse about general selfishness, materialism and abandonment of American values. By the 1890s, one result was a kind of crusade which quickly became known as Progressivism. On the surface, this was just a vigorous reform movement, composed of many elements and with many different goals, and as such its practical successes were not very great. This is usually explained by pointing out that the movement was essentially highly conservative. Optimistic and themselves economically secure, middle-class Progressives were not really committed to dismantling the system. But

Progressive conservatism went a good deal deeper than an instinctive self-interest. The panic of the intellectuals, shared by a significant portion of the movement, was over the deepest implications of the rise of the corporate-industrial society.

The old values, individualism, self-reliance, democratic integrity, to which just about everybody had paid lip-service for most of the century, no longer fitted the new structure. The trouble was, what America most deeply believed about herself, her core values, were inextricably linked to agrarian idealism. What place had free, independent farmers and the purifying force of nature in a world dominated by John D. Rockefeller, the U.S. Steel Corporation and Wall Street bankers? One practical result was strong support for a growing conservation movement. An impractical result was a great deal of talk about getting 'back to nature.' Neither touched the real problem. Now individualism and self-reliance were not merely threatened, they had become for the mass of Americans *irrelevant* in an urban-industrial society.

Behind their front of forward-looking reform, a large portion of middle-class America yearned for a lost, golden past. The Progressives yearned for a world which offered freedom of individual action, not market determinism, had a place for honour, chivalry and nobility of character, not relationships governed by business motives, was Anglo-Saxon, not adulterated with the refuse of Europe, and was revivified by contact with nature, not stultified by the urban-industrial landscape. These Americans burned with guilt and anger over the greed and indifference which had brought about the world they despised – but which gave them an easy prosperity. They wallowed in nostalgia – for a world which had of course never existed.

This is precisely the sort of contradiction which calls up a functional myth to resolve it. Across the Atlantic, some of Britain's middle class were also repelled by industrialism. In a gesture typical of the Victorians, they attempted, of all things, a revival of the Arthurian myth: just as the Christian knight could demonstrate a compromise between the life of the spirit and that of the brutal warrior, so could the Christian gentleman show a middle way between the moral life and the industrial robber baron. The symptoms of this eccentricity were a great deal of posturing about chivalry and a passion for the medieval, all given extra respectability by the poet laureate, Lord Tennyson. There were, surprisingly, some stirrings of interest in importing the Arthurian myth into the United States, though the nearest thing to an exemplar of chivalry had been the 'Southern cavalier,' lost after the Civil War. Mark Twain decisively helped to scupper it in 1889 with *A Connecticut Yankee in King Arthur's Court*, whose main thrust is a contrast between American democracy and feudal tyranny, and whose theme is a diatribe against all nobilities as bloodsucking parasites. Behind the vituperation, Twain had got one thing absolutely right: chivalry was the creed of a privileged class, not the common man, the code of an order, not the guiding principle of a people.* For the United States the Arthurian myth was a quaint and remote irrelevancy. This came as something of a disappointment to a handful of writers and intellectuals who kept on creating echoes of the Arthurian ideal for some time to come – until perhaps they died forever with John F. Kennedy.

If America found her own, native-born myth in the West, this was not a foregone conclusion. Of course, the march westward had been one of the key symbols of progress and Western settlement had been a kind of proof of the validity of agrarian idealism. The West had consistently been romanticised, had generated the nation's most exciting legends and consistently produced heroes. To shape this into a functional myth required a catalyst. Between 1888 and 1902, Theodore Roosevelt, Frederic Remington and Owen Wister convinced a majority of the nation that the qualities which could save America were to be found on the last, vanishing frontier. They had much in common: all three were Easterners and upper-class, were friends and shared a good many attitudes and ideas. Each went West to escape pressures felt to be intolerable; it has been suggested all three, in different ways, suffered trauma involving wife or mother (or both), which shaped their responses to life. Each in fact played at being a Westerner and turned the game into a successful career.

Theodore Roosevelt was born into a wealthy New York patrician family and was educated at Harvard. He had suffered from asthma as a child and was warned when he was twenty-one that he had a weak heart. With what was to become characteristic energy and determination he flung himself into an outdoor lifestyle designed to build up his strength. After his marriage in 1880, he became involved in Republican party activity in New York and was elected on a reform platform to the state legislature in 1882. When his health weakened in 1883, he took a hunting trip to the Dakota Territory and while there decided to buy into a ranching partnership. In February 1884 he suffered a personal tragedy: his wife and his mother died on the same day. Immediately afterwards his political

---

*Theodore Roosevelt noted in 1881: 'The Age of Chivalry was lovely for the knight but it must have at times been inexpressively gloomy for the gentlemen who had to occasionally act in the capacity of daily bread for their betters.'

prospects seemed to suffer a serious reverse, so Roosevelt tidied up his affairs in New York and went to Dakota, where he invested $85,000 in stocking and expanding his Maltese Cross ranch on the Little Missouri River. Though he stayed in Dakota for a year, he was not, as the impression is sometimes given, a recluse. He returned at regular intervals to New York both to see his family and to repair his career in politics. His time as a rancher however was to change his life.

Roosevelt was determined to be accepted by Westerners, ranchers and cowboys alike. His spectacles, high-pitched voice and occasional stilted diction initially had the reverse effect and he was taken as something of a joke.* This impression soon disappeared. In the spring round-up of 1885 he rode one hundred miles a day, stood all-night watches and once remained in the saddle for forty hours. If his stamina was phenomenal, his courage could not be questioned. Several frequently-told stories gave him a reputation. Ordered by a saloon bully with a gun in each hand to buy drinks all round, Roosevelt instantly knocked him down; surprised by a 1200 pound grizzly, he stood his ground and shot it dead at eight paces; and caught in the open by five Indians who threatened him, he coolly scared them off. One incident made him a minor celebrity. In March 1886 he discovered that a small boat, used by the ranch on the Little Missouri, had been stolen by three local horse-thieves, one of whom was known as a gunman. Despite the risk and dreadful weather, Roosevelt and two companions pursued the thieves for thirteen days and caught them. Instead of stringing them up on the nearest tree, as any Westerner would and several later told him he should have done, Roosevelt brought them back, in atrocious conditions, 150 miles to the nearest town with a law officer. By 1886, Roosevelt could claim he been accepted by Westerners: he was chairman of the local cattlemen's association and had been elected delegate to the much larger and more powerful Stockmen's Association of Montana.

Fate, as well as his own intentions, ensured Roosevelt would not remain in Dakota. As it did hundreds of other ranches, the winter of 1886-87 wiped out the Maltese Cross, which lost at least 50% of its cattle. Uncertain of an immediate political career, he had taken positive steps toward becoming a writer. In 1882 he had published a serious historical work and had contributed a number of light pieces to magazines. Between February and June 1888 he published a series of articles in *Century*, immediately republished in book-form as

---

* He is alleged on one occasion to have shouted to a cowboy 'Hasten forward quickly there!'

Ranch Life and the Hunting Trail. At the same time he had begun a four-volume work, eventually published between 1889 and 1896 and entitled *The Winning of the West.*

The latter was greeted with applause by historians and enthusiasm by the public – the first volume was a best-seller. What Roosevelt had offered was a grand historical panorama which reminded Americans of the role of the West in revealing American destiny and racial superiority. In *Ranch Life and the Hunting Trail*, the purposes were much simpler and the results more far-reaching. Roosevelt's intentions were perfectly clear: they were first, to publicise his vision of the West he had personally experienced and second, to publicise himself.

Roosevelt vividly presented a land whose contrast to the East was stressed at every turn. In the West a man will find that

> he lives in the lonely lands…where prairies stretch out into the billowing plains of waving grass girt only by the blue horizon – plains across whose endless breadth he can steer his course for days and weeks and see neither man to speak to nor hill to break the level…

This was a land '… to make a man's blood leap with sheer buoyant light-heartedness and eager, exultant pleasure in the boldness and freedom of the life he is leading.'

And of course the West contained a different breed of men:

> The men of the border reckon upon stern and unending struggles with their iron-bound surroundings; against the grim harshness of their existence they set the strength and abounding vitality that come with it. They run risks to life and limb that are unknown to the dwellers in cities…

Roosevelt reserved his highest praise for the cowboys he had worked with. They were '…as hardy and self-reliant as any men who ever breathed – with bronzed, set faces and keen eyes that look all the world straight in the face without flinching…' In the main they were 'hardworking, faithful fellows' and on the range '…quiet, rather self-contained men, perfectly frank and simple, and on their own ground treat a stranger with the most whole-souled hospitality.' He conceded that they could become drunk and violent but this was '…mere horseplay; it is the cowboy's method of "painting the town red" as an interlude in his harsh monotonous life.' Cowboys had indeed been too often maligned:

> Few of the outrages quoted in the Eastern papers as their handiwork are such in reality, the average Easterner apparently considering every individual who wears a broad hat and carries a six-shooter a cowboy.

With the publication of *Ranch Life and the Hunting Trail*, Roosevelt completed the transformation of the cowboy's image begun by Buffalo Bill Cody and the Eastern press. He then took the process a stage further: noble, courageous and *heroic*, the one-time itinerant agricultural worker on horseback took his place as the heir of Leatherstocking:

...the wild rough rider of the plains should be seen in his own home. There he passes his days, there he does his life work, there, when he meets death, he faces it as he has faced many other evils, with quiet, uncomplaining fortitude. Brave, hospitable, hardy and adventurous he is the grim pioneer of our race; he prepares the way for the civilization from before whose face he must disappear.

Even as Roosevelt displayed his West as the shining example for the nation, he sounded its death-knell. That world, he wrote in 1888:

...must pass away before the onward march of our people; and we who have felt the charm of the life, and have exulted in its abounding vigour and its bold, restless freedom, will not only regret its passing for our own sakes only, but must also feel real sorrow that those who come after us are not to see, as we have seen, what is perhaps the pleasantest, healthiest, and most exciting phase of American existence.

These views on the West and on the cowboy were not those of a dime novelist or any ordinary magazine writer: they were those of a prominent figure in the Eastern establishment. They also carried the awful stamp of authenticity for, as Roosevelt wrote to Richard W. Gilder, the editor of *Century*:

I have been part of all that I describe; I have seen the things and done them; I have herded my own cattle, I have killed my own food; I have shot bears, captured horse-thieves and "stood off" Indians. The descriptions are literally exact; few Eastern men have seen the wild life for themselves.

From 1886 Roosevelt was trying to use his Western experiences as part of a self-promotion campaign. He was narrowly dissuaded, by his sister and friends, from publishing an instant account of the horse-thief episode but, unsurprisingly, the reports in the Dakota press were picked up by the *New York Times*. *Ranch Life and the Hunting Trail* not only included it but identified Roosevelt totally with the hard, exciting and romantic life he described. When he wrote of the cowboy

He possesses, in fact few of the emasculated, milk-and-water moralities
admired by the pseudo-philanthropists; but he does possess, to a very
high degree, the stern, manly qualities that are invaluable to a nation

as much as anything, Roosevelt meant himself.

The rewards were not long in coming. Continuing as a reform
Republican, Roosevelt became a member of the Civil Service Commission in 1889 and in 1897 was appointed Secretary of the Navy in
McKinley's first administration. At the outbreak of the Spanish-
American War in 1898, in a gesture typical of all his qualities, he
resigned to raise a regiment of Westerners to fight in Cuba. The First
U.S. Volunteer Cavalry, of which Roosevelt was second-in-com-
mand, was composed of an extraordinary mixture of his Eastern
friends and cowboys, who volunteered on a ratio of 20 to 1 for places
available. Born for a nickname, the regiment finally settled on
Roosevelt's Rough Riders.* Roosevelt was not a particularly effective officer and the regiment did not see action as a cavalry unit. But
in the crucial battle for Santiago, Roosevelt led his dismounted men
through galling fire up Kettle Hill and on to victory on San Juan
Heights. As a result, the press made him a popular hero and the
Republican party bosses capitalised on his fame to run him successfully for the governorship of New York. Unfortunately for them,
Roosevelt continued as a reformer and his attacks on corruption
became an embarrassment. In desperation the party conservatives
nominated him for the Vice-Presidency in 1900, because the office
notoriously offered no scope for action of any kind. The best laid
plans on this occasion went spectacularly astray, for McKinley was
assassinated in September 1901 and Roosevelt became, as party boss
Mark Hanna is alleged to have said, 'that damned cowboy in the
White House.'

The West made Theodore Roosevelt and he knew it: 'If I had not
spent my year in North Dakota, I never would have become President of the United States.' What he recognised was the way he had
been transformed from an aristocrat to a democrat, how the West
had given him a gift priceless to a politician, the aura of a man of the
people. He acknowledged it publicly in 1910:

I regard my experience during those years, when I lived and worked with
my own fellow-ranchmen on what was then the frontier, as the most

---

* It is usually supposed that Roosevelt took the name from Buffalo Bill Cody's Wild
West act 'Rough Riders of the World' – an assemblage of cowboys, which also
included assorted Mexicans, Cossacks and foreign cavalry units. Roosevelt's own
use of the phrase ten years before in *Ranch Life* suggests it might have had a currency
quite independent of Cody.

important educational asset of my life…I know how the man that works
with his hands and the man on the ranch are thinking, because I have
been there, and am thinking that way myself.

Yet Roosevelt made the West which made him. The frontier which
he described was not the frontier seen with the eye of an unbiased
reporter, but one given almost mystic qualities. Its ugliness and
cruelty were dismissed to the margins and its harshness was praised
as a factor creating the rugged heroes who were held up for national
admiration. And having produced an image of himself as a cowboy
from the cowboys' West, he did not hesitate to manipulate it with a
style that Cody would have admired. When running for Vice-Presi-
dent, Roosevelt hired fake cowboys to chase his campaign train,
firing their pistols; campaigning for the presidency in 1904, he shared
platforms with Buck Taylor; and in 1912, when he ran unsuccessfully
as a Progressive, he displayed Frank James (at 69 years of age!) as
his bodyguard.

The impact of *Ranch Life and the Hunting Trail* was much enhanced
by its illustrations, drawn by the twenty-six year old Frederic Remington. The son of a New York publisher, Remington dropped out of
Yale art school, went to Montana in 1881 and (showing dreadful
judgment for a future artist of cowboys) tried sheep-ranching in
Kansas, then failed as a saloon-keeper in Kansas City. Perhaps partly
to impress his wife and her family, he turned to painting in 1885 and
sold some illustrations to *Harper's Weekly*. He returned to New York
the following year and took classes at the Art Students' League, then
joined General Miles, as a war artist, for the campaign against the
Apache led by Geronimo. When he returned, he sold 31 paintings and
drawings from his portfolio to *Harper's* and shortly after was given the
contract by *Century* to illustrate Roosevelt's articles. From that point
Remington never looked back: within a decade he was the best-known
artist in America. Briefly a war artist in Cuba, his paintings *The
Scream of Shrapnel at San Juan Hill*, and *The Charge of the Rough
Riders at San Juan Hill*, both highlighting Roosevelt, helped make
Roosevelt a national hero. At his premature death in 1909 Remington
had produced over 2750 paintings and drawings and twenty-five
bronzes, as well as a good deal of writing designed to increase the
market for his work as an artist.

Remington claimed that he had appointed himself the visual
historian of a world which he, like Roosevelt, saw disappearing. In
1905 he wrote:

I knew the railroad was coming. I saw men already swarming into the
land. I knew the derby hat, the smoking chimneys, the cord binders and

the thirty-day notes were upon us in a restless surge. I knew the wild riders and the vacant land were about to vanish forever...Without knowing exactly how to do it, I began to try to record some facts around me.

But like Roosevelt, Remington did not record facts; he presented a carefully constructed image coloured by his own convictions. He saw the West as a theatre, and the drama playing was usually a tragedy. Like the theatre, the scenery was not important – Remington made no effort to capture Western landscapes – the play was the thing. What he displayed in his finest pictures was heroism: cavalry in action, cowboys caught in Indian fights or in a stampede. As William Goetzmann has elegantly put it: 'Remington's imaginary frontier was a stoic, existential world of tragedy and violence that resembled the literary world of Ernest Hemingway with its descriptions of bullfighters and tough-guy killers waiting for the end. It was a bleak world of cultural entropy.'

Much of it was a world of Remington's invention. His portraits in a 'procession' of frontier types were vivid – but they contained types, like the 'old-time mountain man,' Canadian trapper and 'old-style Texas cowman' he could never have seen. When after 1889 he turned more and more to cowboy subjects, he claimed great accuracy of detail and brought back a good deal of cowboy riding gear for his studio – but he dressed his cowboys virtually in a uniform, and one that few cowboys actually wore. This assertion is easily tested by comparing Remington's pictures with contemporary photographs. Estelle Jussim has shown that his early drawings were based on L.A. Huffman's photographs (and on those by Roosevelt), but he soon abandoned the camera and relied on his own inner eye. Most art critics praise the results: an infusion of emotion and the capture of dramatic action. But, despite Remington's claims, as drama entered authenticity faded. Close examination of the excellent photographs, for example, of Texas cowboys by Andrew A. Forbes and Wyoming cowboys by Charles D. Kirkland show not a uniform but a wonderful variety of shirts, pants (including jeans) and hats. Some wear chaps and some do not; Remington's almost invariably did, but no photograph shows a cowboy wearing a fancy Mexican jacket, one of Remington's studio props and adorning a cowboy in *A Dash for the Timber*, painted in 1889.

Photographs showed what cowboys really were – hardworking employees in an open-air occupation. Remington painted heroes, often caught in moments of acute danger and often displaying the true hero's hallmark – an act of chivalry. Despite his claims, he was not a reporter but an image-maker and he was painting what his ever-growing success taught him the public wanted to see. Because he was the best-known painter in the United States, his influence was enormous (he created a market for his subject matter that made the careers of half-a-dozen artists who followed him). His role as a myth-maker perfectly complemented that of Roosevelt: if Roosevelt had convinced Americans that the loss of the old life in the West was a national tragedy, Remington showed them what had been lost. But just as Roosevelt manipulated his Western experience for his own ends, so Remington recognised he was marketing a product. In April 1900 he wrote to Owen Wister:

> I am as you know working on a big picture book – of the West and I want you to write a preface...telling the d— public that this is the real old thing – step up and buy a copy – last chance – ain't going to be any more West etc.

In 1893 Remington had met Wister in Yellowstone Park, during the latter's eighth visit to the West, and persuaded him to write a series of articles for *Harper's Monthly Magazine* which Remington would illustrate. Like Remington, Wister was an Easterner and like Roosevelt he was an aristocrat. Wister's father was a Philadelphia doctor but his mother was the daughter of Fanny Kemble, the famous English actress and Pierce Butler, grandson of one of the Founding Fathers; a writer herself, she was to be her son's least flattering critic. Wister read music at Harvard, where he met and became a friend of Roosevelt, and spent a year in Paris studying to become a composer. His father made him return in 1883 and put him to work in a Boston bank. He tried his hand at writing a novel but was advised not to publish it. In 1885 he fell ill; no diagnosis is recorded but it rather looks as if the illness, and its subsequent recurrences, were psychosomatic. To recuperate, Wister went West – to Wyoming, about which Roosevelt had written to him. When he returned he went back to Harvard to read law and in 1888 began a career as an attorney, but each summer for the next fourteen years he returned to the West. In 1891 he decided to write about it.

Many years later, Wister described his motives when he made that decision:

> Why wasn't some Kipling saving the sagebrush for American literature, before the sagebrush and all that it signified went the way of the California forty-niner, went the way of the Mississippi steamboat, went the way of everything? Roosevelt had seen the sagebrush true, had felt its poetry; and also Remington, who illustrated his articles so well. But what was fiction doing, fiction, the only thing that has outlived fact?

In the next few months he sold two stories to *Harper's* and was sent West by the firm in 1893, where he met Remington, who talked him into writing a series to be called 'The Evolution of a Cowboy.' It appeared in 1895, a short-story collection, *Red Man and White* in 1896, a novel entitled *Lin McLean* in 1898 and another collection, *The Jimmyjohn Boss*, in 1900. Two years later Wister published *The Virginian*, which was to become the most famous Western novel ever written. It went through fifteen reprints in eight months, was reprinted 38 times by 1928, when it was in its fifteenth edition. It was turned into a play in 1904 and became a standard repertory item for thirty years; it has been filmed four times and was the (scarcely recognisable) basis for a television series which ran for eight years.

Like Roosevelt and Remington, Wister was an Easterner who had fallen in love with the West, believed it to contain all that was best in America's experience and mourned because that best was disappearing for ever. And like Roosevelt and Remington he claimed he would record its passing. What he recorded of course was his own romantic vision. Wister's West too was a mystical place; he wrote in his journal for 1891: 'After two years, this glorious, this supernatural atmosphere, meets me again better, clearer, more magical, even than I remembered it.' Wister's focus however was the unique qualities of the Westerner, and specifically, the cowboy. The first illustration for 'The Evolution of a Cowboy' showed a cowboy against a background of the world's heroic horsemen and is entitled *The Last Cavalier*; Wister's text read: 'From the tournament to the round-up!...so upon the land has the horse been his foster-brother, his ally, his playfellow, from the tournament of Camelot to the round-up in Abilene.' Those who had been deprived of the knight-errant as an alien import had got him back as a native son.

In fiction, Wister gave cowboys the qualities accorded them by Roosevelt and Remington. What Wister spends a good deal of time describing in these paragons is not so much their qualities as their style – their economy of speech and action, their laconic humour, and their minimalist approach to critical situations. All this is given its best expression in *The Virginian*. Since the plot revolves around the love of a Westerner, who is occasionally described as a young savage, and a schoolteacher, who is an Eastern lady, and conflict over when and whether it is right to take the law into one's own hands, the whole thing has blatantly obvious echoes of James Fenimore Cooper. But the reader need not worry: the cowboy is a natural gentleman and the lady learns that in Wyoming Western values make more sense than Eastern theorising – and the values are what is on display.

Wister's West was a world of wish-fulfilment – it became what he wanted it to be and its heroes were what he wished he was. His background naturally at first made him something of a snob and an Eastern snob at that – on his first visit West in 1885 he was pleased to note that most of those he met came '... from the East, and generally from New England, thank goodness.' His daughter thought it remarkable that he could make friends with cowboys as easily as judges, but his hosts in the West were often people of his own class – men like Major Frank Wolcott, the leader of the Johnson County invasion of 1892. Though he hunted and rode, Wister never aspired to match the feats of Roosevelt nor could he match Roosevelt's instant courage: witness to what he himself described as an atrocious act of cruelty he behaved like a wimp and remained, as he wrote in his journal, '...the moral craven who did not lift a finger or speak a word.' When he wrote the incident into *The Virginian*, the hero beats up the perpetrator. Wister knew perfectly well the West had its dark side; he wrote in his diary entry for 20 June 1891:

> I begin to conclude from five seasons of observation that life in this negligent irresponsible wilderness tends to turn people shiftless, cruel and incompetent. I noticed in ...1885, and I notice today, a sloth in doing anything and everything, that is born of the deceitful ease which makeshifts answer here. Did I believe in the efficacy of prayer, I should petition to be the hand that once and for all chronicled and laid bare the virtues and the vices of this extraordinary phase of American social progress.

When his stories came to be written the vices had a place, but they were overshadowed by the virtues, the towering nobility of the cowboy heroes and the visible superiority of Western values for a decadent and corrupt East. Wister's fictional West shows an alternative: a land of freedom, honesty, and integrity where the mean and the cruel get their just deserts and the wicked perish. His influence was extraordinary. Wister did not just rescue the cowboy from his dead end in dime novels; he created the modern Western. *The Virginian* produced the laconic hero, slow to action but invincible when aroused: 'When you say that, *smile!*' It decreed in fiction for the first time that, in the West at least, a man's gotta do what a man's gotta do: it is no step at all from the exchange between the Virginian and Molly before he goes out to kill the villain Trampas: 'Can't yu' see how it must be about a man?' 'I cannot...if I ought to I cannot;' and Gary Cooper answering Grace Kelly as he turns back to meet the Miller brothers at high noon: 'I've never run from any man before in my life.' 'I don't understand any of this.' 'Well, I haven't got time to tell you...'

Perhaps most significant of all, Wister invented the gunfight. Of course, dime novel fiction was punctuated with shootings and even duels – the essence of the fictional Wild West was that people shot each other with abandon and monotonous regularity. But Wister invented a totally distinctive Western duel: the walkdown, even-break gunfight, down to the proper formalities – the villain gives the hero until sundown to leave town. It was a complete invention, for surviving Western records produce no example of such a ritualised encounter. Most gunfights seemed to have been murderously casual affairs; some start with threats, after which both parties seem at liberty to kill their opponent as occasion offers and without further warning. Some indeed take place in the street but the contestants appear never to square off for a fast draw. The real-life encounter nearest to Wister's fiction might be the fight between Dave Tutt and Wild Bill Hickok on 21 July 1865 in Springfield, Missouri, when both men walked across the town square (and Tutt made the fatal mistake of opening fire at fifty yards). The more common street gunfight was like the one beween Luke Short and James Courtwright in Fort Worth, Texas, on 8 February 1887. Both men walked down the street together and stopped a few feet apart; Short protested he was unarmed, at which Courtwright instantly drew his pistol, which jammed, and Short shot him with the gun he had claimed he did not have.*

These points are not entirely trivial, because Wister's invention of the ritual gunfight is part of a larger imaginary structure – the 'code of the West.' Particularly in *The Virginian*, Wister gave the impression that the chivalry and honour of the cowboy was not merely the expression of an inner purity of spirit, but a well-understood code of behaviour which bound all men in the West – Trampas is a villain not just because he is a rustler, but because he shoots a man in the back. Roosevelt could have told Wister, if he did not know it perfectly well himself, that in the West when it came to shooting there were no rules except the law of self-preservation.

Just as Roosevelt and Remington had done, Wister manufactured a West to point up the values the United States seemed to have abandoned. His political views were clear when he met Remington in 1893:

Remington is an excellent American; that means, he thinks as I do about the disgrace of our politics and the present asphyxiation of all real love of country. He used almost the same words that have of late been in my

---

* This may be the shooting which inspired Remington's *A Fight in the Street.*

head, that this continent does not hold a nation any longer but is merely a strip of land in which a crowd is struggling for riches.

By the time he came to write *The Virginian*, Wister was as much as anything a propagandist. In his preface to the 1911 edition, re-dedicated to Roosevelt, he was explicit:

> If this book be anything more than an American story, it is an expression of American faith. Our Democracy has many enemies, both in Wall Street and in the Labor Unions; but as those in Wall Street have by their excesses created those in the Unions, they are the worst...But I believe...we people will prove ourselves equal to the severest test which political man has yet subjected himself – the test of Democracy.

Roosevelt, Remington and Wister had successfully sold to America a collective vision and they collaborated to sustain it. In his autobiography Roosevelt wrote:

> I have sometimes been asked if Wister's "Virginian" is not overdrawn; why, one of the men I have mentioned...was in all essentials the Virginian in real life, not only in his force but in his charm. Half of the men I worked with or played with and half of the men who soldiered with me afterwards in my regiment might have walked out of Wister's stories or Remington's pictures.

They had offered all the elements of a myth: the West of the cattle ranges held the freedom and the values which the nation needed and the cowboy was its epic hero, the last free individual in a society which had destroyed individualism. All the elements that is save one: the West and the cowboy had been inconvenient enough to die. If the example for redemption was historical, to a nation which had an impatient irreverence for history it might as well be drawn from Ancient Rome as from Wyoming. In the preface to *The Virginian* Wister gave the clue to how the myth might become complete. In as contrived a poetic flight as one can hope to find, he begins by tolling the bell over the corpse of the West in familiar fashion:

> It is a vanished world. No journeys, save those which memory can take, will bring you to it now...So like its old self does the sagebrush seem when revisited, that you wait for the horseman to appear. But he will never come again. He rides in his historic yesterday.

Is this just another reminder of what we can never have again? Not quite, for Wister goes on:

> What is become of the horseman, the cowpuncher, the last romantic figure upon our soil?...Well, he will be here among us always, invisible,

waiting his chance to live and play as he would like. His wild kind has been among us always, since the beginning...

All is not lost! The *spirit* of the cowboy, the values he stood for and the West he represented will survive because he is part of the American character. This is all very poetic, but what was needed to give the myth permanent substance was an intellectual justification for the continuing presence of the lost West in the America of the future. That was provided by an academic historian.

In a supplement to his decennial report for 1890, published in 1892, the Superintendent of the Census had noted in passing that the pattern of Western settlement had reached the point where 'there can hardly be said to be a frontier line.' Since the Census Report was hardly likely to have been compulsive reading for most Americans, the implications of this announcement, startling as they were, might have gone unremarked for some time. It provided however a further stimulus to Frederick Jackson Turner, a thirty-one year old historian at the University of Wisconsin, to bring together the ideas he had been developing on American historical determinants. He presented the results to the American Historical Association at its 1893 meeting in Chicago. 'The Significance of the Frontier in American History' was to become certainly the most famous and probably the most influential historical paper ever delivered in the United States.

For Turner, the West was the key to understanding the uniqueness of American history: 'The existence of an area of free land, its constant recession, and the advance of American settlement westward, explain American development.' In this paper and subsequent elaborations, Turner posed a series of propositions. American institutions were unique because they were constantly forced to adapt to fresh needs emerging from national expansion. American society never solidified into Old World patterns because on each successive frontier it first disintegrated and then reconstituted itself, involving a kind of cyclic social and political renaissance. The easy availability of land and resources permitted independence and encouraged a rejection of excessive interference by external authority. Dealing with the problems of the wilderness was an experience shared by all pioneers alike, so that they were Americanised. Turner thus argued that the frontier had been the generator of democracy, an incubator of individualism and a nationalising factor. To this he later added his version of the notion that the frontier was also a 'safety-valve' for potentially discontented Eastern labour.

In these arguments, Turner had proposed only what the frontier *had* done, and he had begun from the assumption that the closing of the frontier marked the end of the first great phase of American history. But in a famous passage he explained how the effects of the frontier experience were permanent:

> To the frontier the American intellect owes its striking characteristics. That coarseness and strength combined with acuteness and acquisitiveness; that practical and inventive turn of mind, quick to find expedients; that masterful grasp of material things, lacking in the artistic but powerful to effect great ends; that restless, nervous energy; that dominant individualism, working for good and for evil, and withal that buoyancy and exuberance which come with freedom – these are the traits of the frontier, or traits called out elsewhere because of the existence of the frontier.

As far as the myth was concerned, this argument was the clincher: the West was not lost, because the spirit of the frontier was embedded in the American personality for ever.

Turner's original paper did not burst like a bombshell on an amazed and grateful public. Popularising the message took time: Turner pushed its ideas through a series of articles, some for wide readership in journals like the *Atlantic Monthly* and it was helped along by the support of distinguished figures like Woodrow Wilson, professor of Law and Politics at Princeton (and future president). By about 1903 the 'frontier thesis' was known to all professional historians in the United States and its ideas were familiar to many Americans. From that point it simply took off. Turner's biographer, Ray Allan Billington, has shown how from 1910 historians just rewrote all American history in terms of the frontier thesis. Every American history textbook published between 1926 and 1930 centred on the frontier and 80% of the most widely used accepted the thesis as unarguable.

It was of course open to a great deal of argument. In popularising his great idea, Turner had expanded on his original thoughts with more and more speculation. What he did not do was offer much evidence for the thesis – in some cases, none at all – and his growing band of disciples made even more extravagant claims. Eventually, in the 1930s and 1940s, critics began a wholesale demolition of the frontier interpretation. Of the elements which survived, interestingly enough the 'persistence of frontier traits' in the American character, as Ray Billington termed it, seems the most valid. Some of these traits are admirable: a belief in hard work as a guaranteed means of getting on, the expectation of upward mobility, a commitment to egalitarianism. Others might be judged according to the prejudices of the observer, like impatience with culture and anti-intellectualism. Some characteristics bred on the frontier are America's problems: excessive materialism and a casual wastefulness of resources. One frontier trait obvious to contemporaries but invisible in the myth was the indifference to pollution of the environment. Patricia Limerick quotes a Montana housewife commenting on the piles of cans strewn outside every home, and even Wister remarked: 'Houses, empty bottles, and garbage, they were forever of the same shapeless pattern.' As for the *values* of the West, nobility, chivalry, honour, the code of the West, these did not persist because they had never existed anyway as the exclusive distinguishing qualities of the West.

None of this was remotely in the minds of Americans at the turn of the century, for an unambiguous picture had been painted for them. In 1903 it had all come together. Roosevelt was the cowboy in the White House, Remington was America's most popular artist, *The Virginian* was a runaway best-seller and Turner's thesis was becoming widely accepted. The public was hooked on a mythic image of a West whose essence was somehow genetically transmitted. Once adopted, that notion meant that the story of the West moved out of history and the West became a timeless world. There, each successive present could, indeed should, play and replay its conflicts and dilemmas within a framework and according to rituals accepted as a matter of faith.

Chapter Six

The West's Response

Well, maybe we didn't talk that way before Mr. Wister wrote his book, but we sure all talked that way after the book was published.

Anonymous cowboy

I'm being paid to lie about the West. I'm going back home where I can do honest work.

Maynard Dixon, 1912.

...the free-running reprobate...becomes a very hero of democracy

Emmett Dalton, 1931.

There is, wrote Kipling, nothing quite so terrible as an idea whose time has come. In the first decade of the twentieth century the myth of the West did not merely flourish: it escaped the hands of its creators and became entrenched in the collective unconscious of America. To some cynical contemporaries public passion for the West looked no more than a craze, and in some areas the cynics were right. A fad for Western plays engendered by the success of *The Virginian* on stage died out about 1908. But Western drama just switched to the cinema, a medium which would eventually reach audiences immeasurably larger than the theatre's. The film industry in turn relied for its scripts, as it would in all genres indefinitely, on novels and Western novels were the literary growth industry of the era. Frank H. Spearman published the first of his Whispering Smith stories in 1906, Clarence E. Mulford created Hopalong Cassidy and the Bar 20 in 1907 and Eugene Manlove Rhodes began his career as a Western novelist with *Good Men and True* in 1910. Emerson Hough had written a history of the cowboy as early as 1897 and published his first novel before *The Virginian*, but reached his peak with

Covered Wagon in 1922 and *North of '36* the following year.

None of these writers approached anywhere near the popularity of Zane Grey. From 1912 to his death in 1939 Grey produced 78 novels which have sold over twenty million copies and he can well be considered the most successful of all Western authors. Though Frederick Faust, under the pseudonym of Max Brand, was to write hundreds more stories than Grey, and the modern writer Louis L'Amour has over seventy titles and an estimated 100 million copies sold to his credit, a score of Grey's novels are still in print half a century after his death and forty-nine of them have been made into films, twenty-eight of them more than once. Like Wister, Grey was another outsider who (after his first visit to Utah in 1907) became infatuated with the West. But where Wister had offered a West of chivalry and romance, Grey in addition managed to mix together the old belief in the wilderness as a purifying force with Darwinian natural selection, and then offered the Westerner as an evolutionary masterpiece.

Some of the new authors, like Mulford, Hough and Rhodes, gave their heroes a great many human weaknesses. This, it has been claimed, suggests that the unregenerate cowboy of pre-1886 survived the arrival of the mythic hero. Nevertheless, most Western writers, whatever their pretentions to 'realism,' followed Wister down the road to romantic idealism in the sagebrush. Hough put women on the range, Rhodes put his heroes on the wrong side of the law only to highlight their chivalry and nobility. More important, Grey's version of the myth was the one which sold – and his plots ran to a rigid formula, his cardboard characters had relationships unknown in the adult world and his heroes were models of rugged rectitude.

The result was a set of conventions which more or less defined the Western hero for the next fifty years. Opinions might differ on what should be included in the set, but the ground rules would certainly require the following: the cowboy hero is an arrested adolescent (indeed, in his attitude to sex, a pre-adolescent!); he is however invariably kind to women, children and animals, although, as Wayne Michael Sarf has remarked, not necessarily in that order; he instinctively knows the right course of action, not least because he is programmed by the code of the West; and he is a gunman who is the agent of retribution. It was Grey in his first novel, *Riders of the Purple Sage*, who took the next step from *The Virginian* and in 1912 put the gunfighter-hero into fiction, two guns, proper stance and fast draw:

"Look!" hoarsely whispered one of Tull's companions. "He packs two black-butted guns – low down" ... "A gun-man!" whispered another.

"Fellers, careful now about movin' your hands"...The rider dropped his sombrero and made a rapid movement, singular in that it left him somewhat crouched, arms bent and stiff, with the big, black gunsheaths swung round to the fore...

By any rational standards, all this was absurd. It was one thing to argue that the West offered a life of freedom unknown to the industrial cities and therefore to be admired. It was quite another then to give that West, as Roosevelt and Wister did, a general moral superiority, so that it and it alone embodied the values once shared by all America, and could now act as a shining beacon to a nation sinking into darkness. To make an itinerant agricultural worker an epic hero was to create a cultural curiosity. Then to insist that this hero have the maturity of a retarded teenager, the moral outlook of a Sunday School teacher and the skills of an assassin was bizarre. The power of myth however has little to do with reason.

Absurdity did not confine itself to the fabric of the myth. For the most part, the mythic West had been invented by Easterners for Easterners – yet the real West, the West of farmers, miners, business-men, new townships and growing cities, with all its successes and failures, was alive and well. The cattleman's West was passing into history, but ranchers and cowboys lived and were witnesses to what had passed. Why then did the myth not die stillborn in the face of a chorus of ridicule from the real West, proud of its practical achieve-ments? The answer is simple: virtually from the beginning the real West took the myth and solemnly endorsed it.

Nobody benefited from this more than the cowboy. Westerners, some of them former cowboys turned writer, robustly defended the heroic image. Emerson Hough, who in 1897 wrote *The Story of the Cowboy* during his fourth year in New Mexico, began by offering a defence against charges dead a decade before – '...the cowboy has been freely pictured as an embodiment of license and uproarious iniquity' and then continued that he '...is the most gallant modern representative of a human industry second to very few in antiquity.' Twenty-five years later Philip Ashton Rollins, himself a former cowboy, published what purported to be a factual account of the life and work of the ranch-hand. He began by paying tribute to Hough and complaining that after the damage done by the theatre, novels and magazine illustrators, the movies had kept up the bad work – and then promptly went on to aver: 'The cowboy was far more than a theatric character. He was an affirmative, constructive factor in the social and political development of the United States.' Thereafter chapter follows chapter detailing the cowboy's character

('...universality of courage was an earmark of the cowboy's trade...the puncher rarely complained...he was no quitter') through his distinctive speech, his equipment and his dress.

About half-way, Rollins casually remarks that there were '...no typical cowboys.' In 1900 Eugene M. Rhodes, a writer whose views have been deferred to because of his experience in New Mexico, had the hero of his first novel spell it out:

> In the first place take the typical cowboy. There positively ain't no sich person! Maybe so half of 'ems from Texas and the other half from anywhere and everywhere else. But they're all alike in just one thing – and that is that everyone of them is entirely different from all the others.

This is a great relief: for a moment one might have suspected that individualism had faded into a numbing conformity. But no, it was entirely coincidental that all cowboys were brave, uncomplaining, hardworking, laconic, reserved with strangers, hospitable, chivalrous, possessed of a unique sense of humour – and all dressed the same.

As much as anything, the cowboy was his visual image and that image became fixed. Why did the cowboy wear his uniquely distinctive outfit? Richard W. Davis, reporter and managing editor of *Harper's Weekly*, had the audacity to suggest in an account of his trip West in 1892 '...one suspects he wears the strange garments he affects because he knows they are most becoming.' Nonsense, of course! Just about everyone who wrote about the cowboy explained his dress was one hundred percent functional. Most typical were the high-heeled boots, which made walking any distance impossible; naturally, they were to ensure, amid all the hazardous riding, that the foot could not slip through the stirrup. Alfred Lewis, author between 1897 and 1908 of the popular 'Wolfville' tales and self-proclaimed expert on the strength of one visit to Arizona and a law practise in Kansas City, explained they were to '...dig into the ground and hold fast to mother earth while roping on foot.' Both reasons make sense, which is doubtless why later Rollins gave both and, imitating most of those who had written before him, argued the functional utility of the broad-brimmed hat, chaps, the Western saddle, and the rest of the cowboy's accoutrements. If the cowboy wore a uniform, it was simply dictated by the needs of the range.

Several factors need explaining. Contemporary photographs show first, that cowboys seem to change a good deal in general appearance over twenty years, second, there appear to be differences between cowhands in the Southwest and those in the Northwest, third, apart from the broad-brimmed hat, there seems to be a bewildering variety of clothing at any given moment. Emerson Hough flatly pronounced: 'In the cowboy country the fashions of apparel do not change...he is clad today as he was when he first appeared upon the plains.' The evidence suggests otherwise. In 1898 former cowboy W.S. James wrote a short autobiography of his time in Texas. Up to 1877, he comments, '...high-heeled boots were all the rage, and when it was possible to have them, the heel was made to start under the foot, for what reason I never knew, unless it was the same motive that prompts girls to wear the opera heel in order to make a small track, thus leaving the impression that a number ten was a number six...' In 1878 however 'the cow-man had in many places adopted the box-toed boot with sensible heels.'

Riding gear too changed. Back at the beginning of the trail drives in 1867, James says, saddles were high in front with a broad, flat horn and narrow stirrups; by 1872 stirrups were broad but they narrowed again in 1878 with the introduction of the California saddle and its lengthened stirrup straps. This piece of technology, 'taking the place of all others' James notes, was the one which permitted the rider to rest his weight in the stirrup while keeping his seat, so that '...it has been fully demonstrated that a man who rides thus...is capable of riding further and with less fatigue...' Indeed, but it apparently took eleven years for this essential piece of equipment to be adopted – by which time the Texas trail drives were largely over.

The arrival in the mid-1880s of squads of young Easterners and foreigners on the range, particularly in the Northwest, had its own effect. These young men had been attracted by the romantic image currently circulating: they knew what cowboys looked like and they made sure they dressed the part. Their picture must have come from reading matter and the sudden flood of flattering illustrations accompanying it, but in part too it very likely came from Buffalo Bill Cody's Wild West. Cody dressed his cowboys with flamboyance and touches of that flamboyance became common on the range. These young men, unlike the regular range hands, might well be able to afford better quality and the proper style. The newcomers also managed to put a dent into a cherished part of the growing legend. As William Savage has pointed out, the fabled skills with horse and rope, either a Texas birthright or the result of years of practice, these tenderfeet learned in a few weeks. By the implicit admission of the old hands, it could not have been otherwise, for no ranch foreman would have tolerated incompetence for long.

Most contemporaries agreed that, once in town, cowboys blew a portion of their hard-earned pay on store-bought clothes and when they did so they indulged fashion and fancy as much as they pleased. Often as not, they then had their pictures taken in one of the photography studios which seemed to mushroom in every Western township in the 1880s.* One thing is virtually guaranteed, whatever outfit the cowboys are sporting, they are wearing a gun, indeed, quite often holding one. In this they were no different from many badmen, plenty of whom liked the camera, and for the same reason – they knew what image was expected of them. Though of course the 1873 Colt Army model, in its various forms, was not ubiquitous in the West by any means, the range of exotic pistols (with the problems of finding a suitable supply of ammunition which they imply) which turn up in posed portraits suggests that a good many of these firearms were studio props. Does this indicate that cowboys may well have not had guns of their own?

This heretical thought is difficult to substantiate from the welter of contemporary evidence, including photographs. Writing at thirty years' distance from the great days on the range, Rollins firmly argued that pistols were carried only when the cowboy anticipated personal danger or the need to kill animals, when visiting town or calling on a girl. It is well-known that Kansas trail towns passed ordinances against the wearing of firearms within city limits, as did the Territory of New Mexico; (it is not known how the girls reacted.) Did cowboys borrow photographers' props because they had to leave their own gun behind or because they did not have one in the first place? Just about everybody seems to agree that, from the '60s to the '90s Texans and their pistols were inseparable. Hough comments that '...say in 1887, on some ranges not so wild as the far Southwestern country, there was slowly growing a sentiment against the wearing of a "gun".' Photographs of Wyoming cowboys tend to bear him out, but not entirely – some pictures suggest that more cowboys are wearing pistols. Richard Davis probably put his finger on why; like much else the sixgun was a matter of style and cowboys knew what was expected of them:

> His cartridge belt and revolver are on some ranches superfluous, but cattle-men say that they have found that on the days when they took this toy away from their boys, they sulked and fretted and went about their work half-heartedly, so they believe it pays better to humour them...

The growth of the myth ensured that former cowboys began to believe that they had indeed been part of a special brotherhood, that

---

* The bulk of the action of the West's most famous gunfight actually took place near Fly's Photograph Gallery and Studio: somehow the name does not have quite the same ring to it as the nearby O.K. Corral.

the long drive had been a knightly quest and that their experience had marked them out as men who had participated in a glorious adventure. Their autobiographies are shot through with these assumptions. Few go as far as Nat Love, a black cowboy who claimed to be the original Deadwood Dick and wrote his story in 1907 as if it were a dime novel. The best account of a trail drive, by general agreement, is what today would be termed 'faction' – Andy Adams's fictional but accurate *The Log of a Cowboy*, published in 1903. But of those who praise Adams for his realism, and they began with Emerson Hough, few admit the result. Stripped of gunfights, battles with Indians and the usual fantasies and confined to the hazards of nature and the vagaries of men and cattle, *Log of a Cowboy* is just about as interesting as an account of a long sea voyage and about as romantic as the harvest on an Iowa wheat farm.

When George W. Saunders in 1920 called on the old-time trail hands to write up their reminiscences, not all were caught up in the rosy glow. G.O. Burrows remembered well enough '…going hungry, getting wet and cold, riding sorebacked horses, going to sleep on herd and loosing [sic] cattle, getting cussed by the boss…' Of course, he added, all this was forgotten once back in Texas for a spree – but when the life was over, what had he to show for it?

> I always had the "big time" when I arrived in San Antonio rigged out with a pair of high-heeled boots and striped pants and about $6.30 worth of other clothes…I put in eighteen or twenty years on the trail and all I had in the final outcome was the high-heeled boots, the striped pants and about $4.80 worth of other clothes…

Frank Collinson began work on a Texas ranch in 1872 when he was seventeen. In 1874 he took part in a trail drive from Texas to the Sioux reservation in Colorado, then under the supervision of General Custer, (he claimed this was the drive which pioneered the trail to the northern ranges). He began writing up his memories when he was seventy-nine. Distance had not lent enchantment to the view:

> 'When I recall that long cattle drive to the Northwest and think of the hardships we experienced, I wonder if there was really much glamour or adventure to the trip. It was 98 per cent hard work.'

But Collinson then added, with a tepid judiciousness which betrays his origins (he was born in England): '…but I am glad I had the experience…'

Such men were traitors to the cause. In the West the general reaction to the East's vision was one of reverence and the original myth-makers became objects of veneration themselves. Wister quoted a cowboy saying of Roosevelt:

> By God, I never seen anything like it. It was the quickest thing I ever seen...I'm here to tell you that Teddy Roosevelt was the best roper that ever hit that country. I never seen a man that could rope a horse like he did.

If this is true, Roosevelt himself must have been engaging in a moment of modesty – unique in his career – when he wrote, 'I never became a good roper, nor more than an average rider, according to ranch standards.' Wister too was to become revered, as response to *The Virginian* vividly shows. In 1911 Wister took his family to the West on a camping holiday in Wyoming. His daughter later wrote: 'Everybody in the West seems to have read The Virginian, and as soon as they heard my father's name would speak to him about it.' Wister was then apparently regarded as an authority, for Fanny adds: 'The guides talked endlessly to him, asking him questions about the old West.' Particularly gratifying for Wister was the way Westerners found *The Virginian* to be authentic (Cooper plotline, sentimentality, code of the West and all). He made it quite clear that the character of the Virginian himself was a composite of several men he had been acquainted with, but noted: '...within six months of the book's appearance, letters – half a dozen at least – had come to me in which each writer was quite sure he knew who the "original" of the Virginian was – and it was never the same original, nor were any of them known to me.'

This is intriguing, for the Virginian, as a character in the novel's display of the superiority of the West, is in fact a cop-out on Wister's part. He is not a typical cowboy at all, for his superior talents make him first ranch foreman, then his employer's partner and finally a businessman with extensive interests. The Virginian is a yuppie of the range, able to meet head on and compete in the civilisation whose arrival is destroying the old West. The book's typical cowboys have many of the mythic virtues, but they are also casual and feckless, lacking focus and purpose to their lives, losers to be swept away by civilisation's advance. How interesting that Westerners knew the Virginian, but did not rush to claim acquaintance with Lin McLean, Scipio – or Steve whose weakness leads to his lynching as a rustler!

As for cowboys themselves, they appear to have taken the book to their hearts. In the habit of critics everywhere, the Eastern reviewers eventually repented of their early unbridled enthusiasm and began to carp at the novel's supposed realism, picking for example on the dialect Wister made his characters speak. They found no joy

in the West: one cowboy is alleged to have said: 'Well, maybe we
didn't talk that way before Mr. Wister wrote his book, but we sure
all talked that way after it was published.' Fanny Kemble Wister
made the decisive comment on the *The Virginian* in a single phrase:
'It was written as fiction but has become history.'

The West's endorsement of the myth did not confine itself to
novels. The drawings for the first illustrated edition of *The Virginian*
were by Charles Russell, by that point competing with Remington
as a popular artist of the last frontier. Unlike Remington however,
Russell was a Westerner and had actually been a cowboy. He began
working on a sheep ranch in Montana, but sensibly abandoned this
disgraceful occupation, joined a surviving mountain man for two
years and then between 1882 and 1893 worked as a ranch-hand. In
1893 Russell decided to turn his long habit of sketching and painting
into a career as a professional artist and began selling paintings to
Montana saloons; twelve years later his work was being displayed in
New York and he was known nationwide.

Russell's art did not aim for the high drama and the implicit tragic
vision of Remington; he was essentially offering entertainment. Because the development of the sketches and paintings of his cowboy
friends into big canvases drew on life, Russell is usually regarded as
offering the genuine West of his youth – exciting, of course, but with
the indelible stamp of authenticity. His choice of subjects show that
he was playing to the gallery, his themes designed to strike an
already-familiar chord in the public mind. Lonn Taylor has pointed
out that the image of cowboys bursting into town, guns blazing, first
created by Rufus Zogbaum for *Harper's Weekly* in 1886, was im-
itated by Remington three years later and surfaced again, adapted a
little, in Russell's *In Without Knocking* in 1909. Scenes from the
cowboy's work, like *The Broken Rope* (1904), or *A Tight Dally and
Loose Latigo* (1920) show furious action in the face of danger. When
it came to his paintings of cowboys enjoying a little relaxation in
town, the titles give the game away: *Death of a Gambler* (1904),
Smoke of a .45 (1908), *When Guns Speak, Death Settles Disputes*
(1909). Russell covered scores of subjects, but his most popular
paintings (witness their frequency of reproduction) were deliberately
aimed to remind the nation of what it already knew – that the West
was wild.

That image was sustained by artists who reached the vast readership of the new illustrated magazines, like the *Saturday Evening Post*,
Collier's, and *McClure's*, using the new photographic method of
reproducing pictures. Those illustrating the flood of Western stories
were all drama and violence. One of the artists, Maynard Dixon, was

a Westerner, a Californian in fact, and should have known better. He began illustrating for *Harper's Weekly* in 1902 and then developed, for *Sunset Magazine*, a new style of simplified line and colour for Western subjects. So far, so good: but Dixon then moved to New York, the headquarters of magazine publishing, where he could earn far more for his work. There he became trapped in the commercialisation of the myth and committed to connive at the ever-growing romanticisation of the West. Finally, in 1912, he had the courage to declare: 'I'm being paid to lie about the West. I'm going back home where I can do honest work.'*

In its enthusiastic endorsement of the myth, the West eventually had to face up to its own unique contribution to American folklore – the badman. Forward-looking Western businessmen, civic leaders and most of those in the West who saw things in terms of 'progress' were usually embarrassed by the attention given by the press, particularly in the East, to outlaws and gunmen. The West had long since happily validated the results of the Eastern habit of turning obscure figures, like Boone and Carson, into heroes of the frontier. By the 1920s, in a process more remarkable than the canonisation of the cowboy, the West had connived at the extension of this process to the badman.

In September 1908 *Harper's Weekly* published an encapsulated history of Western banditry by Barton W. Currie. The recent exploits of a robber who had held up sixteen stagecoaches in Yellowstone Park prompted Currie to begin by remarking that it '…gives the lie to those who are constantly reminding us that there is naught left that is wild and woolly in the West.' He continued, '…wherefore the lone bandit is a fellow not altogether without merit, having furnished a thrill in days that were dull and heavy with politics' (presumably referring to the presidential election contest between Roosevelt's successor Taft and the orator William Jennings Bryan). The article then reviews the life and times of the Wild Bunch, 'There were thirty…outlaws all, murderers most of them' led by Kid Curry. Butch Cassidy and the Sundance Kid fled with their ill-gotten gains to Europe. Of Billy the Kid Barton writes: 'With the band of desperadoes he led, he raided ranches, "shot up" towns, killed, burned houses and committed outrage after outrage with the blind recklessness of a maniac.' Such was his power as a bandit chief that '…in New Mexico…half the cattlemen paid the youthful desperado tribute.' The Kid was finally hunted down by Pat Garrett, 'that fearless

---

* He did. Dixon later became justly renowned for his evocative rendering of Indians and landscapes.

gunfighter and gambler,' who shot him in the dark as the Kid called out 'Quien va' (quaintly translated as 'Who comes there?'), whereafter he was buried at Fort Stanton. As for the Kid's score as a killer: '...were you to go by the most conservative chronicles, you could put his killings at thirty and have a safe margin for your conscience.'

Continuing the catalogue, through the Apache Kid and Sam Bass, Currie turns to the exploits of Jesse James, detailing his successful defiance of Pinkerton detectives and his death at the hands of Bob Ford. Frank James, against whom no crime was ever proven, '...is still living, a respected business man in St. Louis,' while Bob Ford 'died a tramp.' 'From 1870 until he was assassinated in 1881,' Currie wrote, '...Jesse James was probably the most notorious outlaw in the world. In England, as well as America, the shilling shocker has helped to make his name a household word...Yet today ...[his] evil fame and numberless train robberies are almost forgotten.' Currie concludes solemnly by noting, 'Of all,the criminals I have enumerated scarcely two per cent. died with their boots off.'

The significance of this piece is simple: it is a mirror of contemporary beliefs about Western badmen. Half way through, Currie asserts: 'This is not penny-dreadful fiction, but authenticated fact:' in something over four thousand words it is difficult to find a dozen factually correct statements. The Wild Bunch varied in size but its core averaged about six; Curry was a member but its leader was George Leroy Parker, aka Butch Cassidy, whose claim that he never shot anyone appears to be true. Whether he was killed in Bolivia with the Sundance Kid sometime between 1908 and 1911, or returned to the United States to die peaceably in 1937 (as relatives have alleged), he did not end up, as Currie has it '...in the Paris slums [slain by] those other Apaches of the Rue Pirouette.'

Billy the Kid was one of the small-time gunmen involved, from 1878 to 1880, on the losing side of the fight in Lincoln County, New Mexico, between the Tunstall- McSween faction and members of the Santa Fe Ring. He never led an outlaw gang, in the sense of the James gang or the Wild Bunch, though after Tunstall's murder in 1878 he was one of a group of 'regulators' declared outlaws by the territorial governor, who supported the Ring. The Kid's only involvement in houseburning was as a victim – he was one of those trapped in McSween's house when it was fired by his enemies. After McSween's death the Kid and a handful of the regulators continued sporadic killings, combined with cattle rustling, but so far from running an extortion racket he could not even force McSween's one-time ally John Chisum to pay him for his services as a regulator. Patrick Floyd Garrett had a dubious background (he may have helped the Kid in earlier rustling activities) but does not, prior to killing the Kid in July 1881, appear to have had any particular reputation as a gunman. As for the Kid's reputation, he can only be proved to have killed four men in the whole of his life. It seems curious that Currie should have the Kid buried at Fort Stanton instead of Fort Sumner but extraordinary to have got wrong the most famous last words in Western history: as three witnesses testified and innumerable accounts reported, the Kid cried 'Quien es?'*

In this concatination of misinformation, the section on Jesse James alone is relatively accurate. Indeed Frank James had been acquitted of all charges after his surrender in October 1882, though to describe him as a 'respectable business man' is stretching things somewhat: he never found a steady job thereafter and in 1903 had briefly joined Cole Younger, who had been paroled from the life sentence he had been given in 1877, in a Wild West show. Bob Ford was shot in the saloon of which he was part-owner in 1892. Jesse James however was indeed 'the most notorious outlaw in the world.' What is curious, for it is the only point at which Currie does not reflect current public thinking, is his remark that the James's are 'almost forgotten' in 1908. A very popular biography, first published in 1880, had seen its fourth edition in 1893 and a fifth would be published in 1914. The stream of dime novels starring the bandits, issued by Frank Tousey and Street and Smith from 1881 and numbering 277 in total, had only ceased publication in 1903 – a result of public complaints that they were glorifying crime. Melodramas about the gang had been touring with repertory companies for twenty years and the best of them, *The James Boys in Missouri,* had done excellent business as recently as 1902 in Kansas City. More strikingly, it was made into a film by the Essanay company in 1908.

What explains Currie's extraordinary mixture of fact and fantasy? Clearly, stories about the badmen had, over about thirty years, started to assume legendary proportions, yet these inflated tales were generally and uncritically credited as 'authenticated fact.' It is sometimes assumed that the fault for this lies with the West which, with a kind of perverse pride, invented the badman hero, wove legends about him and foisted the result on a credulous East. The truth is more nearly the opposite – it was the East which in most cases invented the legends, but not necessarily heroic ones. It is clear for example from Currie's piece that the only men who qualify as heroes

---

* Folktales had the Kid buried in several places, despite the statements of Garrett and his deputies; in no time, of course, legend said he was not dead at all. Much has been made, by writers who care to seek poignant significance in the trivial, of Billy meeting death with the question 'Who is it?'

were the lawmen, notably Pat Garrett. The bandits and killers are accorded a kind of ironic admiration for the sheer scale of their iniquities but, with the possible exception of the Jameses, their deserts are seen as just. Yet twenty years after this article appeared in *Harper's* Western gangsters and killers were being paraded as heroes and as part of the myth, and this time it was Western writers who were responsible.

The literary rehabilitation of the frontier psychopath began early. In 1865 George Ward Nichols, writing for *Harper's*, met James Butler Hickok in Missouri and fabricated a biographical piece which was published in February 1867. Nichols invented not only a heroic scout for the Union in the Civil War but also the cool and deadly gunfighter and marksman of awesome skill. Hickok had indeed scouted for the Union during the war, after which he had divided his time between gambling for a living and more scouting. In March 1867 while on campaign he was interviewed by H.M. Stanley (the future finder of Dr. Livingstone). The resultant article, published in the *St. Louis Democrat*, contained the memorable exchange: 'I say, Mr. Hickok, how many white men to your certain knowledge have you killed? After a little deliberation, he replied, "I suppose I have killed considerable over a hundred."' At that point Hickok's total score was two: he had killed David C. McCanles in 1861 and Davis Tutt just before he met Nichols. These pieces, whole or fragmented, were reprinted in scores of papers and made Wild Bill Hickok a nationally-known name.

After acting very briefly as a deputy U.S. marshal in 1868, Hickok served as sheriff of Ellis County, Kansas for four months in 1869 and in 1871 was appointed marshal of Abilene for eight months. He spent most of his time in office gambling and chasing prostitutes and during this period brought his tally of provable killings to a final total of six, one of which was the accidental shooting of one his deputies in Abilene. After this he appears rapidly to have gone down hill to the point of being regarded as a vagrant when he moved to Wyoming in 1874. Some evidence suggests that his eyesight was failing, possibly from VD-related ophthalmia. In 1876 he tried gambling in the new gold-strike centre, Deadwood, and was shot from behind by an assailant whose motives have never been satisfactorily explained.* On these foundations a heroic legend was erected.

Western newspapers had been scornful of the Nichols article, judiciously approving of Hickok's conduct as a lawman and con-

---

* Jack McCall was not avenging a brother slain by Hickok, because he had no brother; no evidence supports his claim that he was hired by a rival gambler.

temptuous of his latter decline. In 1880 however a St. Louis journalist, J.W. Buel, published *The Life and Marvellous Adventures of
Wild Bill*... This (literally) incredible farrago of nonsense combined
all the existing tales about Hickok with a series of wonderful
inventions to illustrate his daring, courage and superhuman skill as
a gunman. It also established Wild Bill as the right kind of hero: he
was the new agent of civilisation on the frontier, imposing order on
the cowtowns with two ivory-handled forty-fours. This image was
repeated by subsequent biographers up to the end of the century.

If Eastern journalists began the process of turning Hickok into
the stalwart foe of frontier crime, they turned Billy the Kid into a
monster of criminal evil. New Mexico papers gave the Kid a prominent part in the Lincoln County War and attributed to him some
killings for which he was not responsible. In the last months of his
life they portrayed him as a ruthless murderer and referred to him
at his death as a common cutthroat. The New York papers took up
Western reports that the Kid had killed a man for every one of his
twenty-one years and established the statement as fact. The *Police
Gazette* published several items in its usual blood-curdling style and
on the Kid's death devoted Number One of its special supplements
on 'Lives and Deaths of Famous Criminals' to him. A Philadelphia
paper produced a story of the Kid living with his gang in a castle
attended by Mexican houris, a theme taken up by some of the
fifteen dime novels featuring him written between 1878 and 1906.

The first Billy biography was published within a year of his death,
ostensibly by Pat Garrett, though it was written, from conversations
with Garrett, by Ashmun Upson. A former reporter for the *New
York Herald*, Upson had come to New Mexico in 1864 and had
worked on local papers. He had briefly acted as Adjutant-General
for the Territory, but resigned after getting into financial difficulties.
He then became postmaster at Caswell, a notary public with involvement in local surveying and then a justice of the peace. As a friend
of Garrett, he wrote *The Authentic Life of Billy the Kid* as a favour;
the book of course entirely belied its title. It was basically designed
to show off a heroic Garrett and was a straightforward exercise in
legend-manufacture; it also incidentally argued that the Kid was
motivated not by bloodlust but revenge for the murder of his patron
Tunstall. Because the book was badly marketed, it did not much
influence public opinion at the time. It was however to influence a
number of other writers, the first of whom was Charles Siringo, who
devoted a chapter to the Kid in *A Texas Cowboy* and saw him as
having some redeeming qualities. Until the turn of the century
however, as Kent L. Steckmesser has shown, the predominant view

of the Kid was that displayed by Emerson Hough – a 'wild beast' with 'the brand of Cain upon his brow.'

The images of the badman generated by writers are easily explained: they simply followed prevailing attitudes to the frontier. In the 1880s the dominant view was the one exploited by Buffalo Bill Cody – the frontier was the meeting point between savagery and civilisation and frontier heroes were the men who subdued the savagery. The focus however had shifted. Previous frontier-tamers had fought savagery in the wilderness to allow the coming of the settlements, but on the last frontier the settlements themselves were wild. Where Boone, Carson and Cody had blazed trails, fought Indians, led settlers and guided the Army, Hickok, who was credited with most of those too, was lauded for *imposing* the first criterion of civilisation – order. Stephen Tatum has pointed out exactly the same attitude explains the vilification of Billy the Kid and the heroification of Garrett. To the East, the Kid represented the forces of barbarism on the frontier, Garrett the forces of progress. Faced with these imperatives, simple things like facts became irrelevant.

One badman however followed a different path to immortality. Jesse James, prince of bandits and the Robin Hood of the West, was invented by Western journalists catering for different public needs. Major John N. Edwards began the process with a piece in the *Kansas City Times* in September 1872, reporting the hold-up of the Kansas City Fair by the James gang. Far from condemning the crime, Edwards wrote: 'It was as if they came from the storied Odenwald, and showed us how things were done that poets sing of.' Edwards, omitting to note that one of the gang's poetic deeds was to shoot a child, went on to appoint the James brothers as the misunderstood knights-errant of the border. In article after article and a biography in 1877, he laboured to show the Jameses as driven to their deeds, acting in self-defence and at all times men of chivalry. Steckmesser has shown how on to these exotic roots was grafted the legend of Jesse as the American Robin Hood. Not content with fabricating half of Hickok's legend, the indefatigable J.W. Buel painted Jesse as a helper of the poor, while the biographies of J.A. Dacus and Frank Triplett (in 1880 and 1882) stressed how the Jameses were victims of political persecution.

Jesse's habit of passing on some of his ill-gotten gains to the poor – paying off widow's mortgages and the like – seems to originate with the ballad which appeared at his death:

Jesse James was a lad who killed many a man
He robbed the Glendale train

He stole from the rich and he gave to the poor
He'd a hand and a heart and a brain.

- none of which did him any good when he was betrayed by
'...Robert Ford, that dirty little coward.' Folktales then proliferated
to show Jesse as pure-hearted, wily and a true friend to the underdog.
Some of these stories actually link back to inventions in the biographies, the rest seem to be folk-memories of the clever-hero champi-
ons of medieval Europe, from Robin Hood to Till Eulenspiegel.

There is not a single scrap of evidence to show that Jesse James
ever gave a cent to the poor. There is on the other hand a great deal
of evidence to suggest that he was a cold-blooded, murderous thief,
who in the course of his crimes did not hesitate to shoot down anyone
who appeared to pose the smallest threat. The original James-Youn-
ger gang was destroyed on its disastrous raid on Northfield, Minnesota, in 1876. The raid was botched and the local citizenry turned
out in force, shot the gang to pieces and pursued and captured most
of them – Jesse and Frank James narrowly escaping. This episode
incidentally does not reflect well on the inhabitants of the Kansas
and Missouri towns in their efforts to deal with the gang in the
previous four years.

The James gang in part survived as long as it did because of the
tacit support of local small farmers, who found little fault in preying
on banks charging crippling interest rates and railroads ruthlessly
exploiting the market. Perhaps more important, during the Reconstruction years after the Civil War, Missouri was a bitterly divided
state. Southern Democrats fighting the power of Radical Republicans found it convenient to present the Jameses as unsurrendered
Southern guerrillas. They thus pressed for an amnesty for the brothers and were frustrated only when Thomas Crittenden, a Democrat
Unionist in the pocket of the railroads, was appointed governor in
1881 and made a deal with Bob Ford to end the problem expedi-
tiously.

There were thousands of ex-Confederates who had as much reason to become bandits as the Jameses but did not (some made a point
of saying so publicly). Nevertheless, parts of the post-Civil War West
regularly saw political power captured by an interest – which therefore also controlled law enforcement. Under such circumstances
definitions of crime became fluid. Richard White has shown that
such conditions existed not only in Missouri but also in Oklahoma
in the 1890s, where the Dalton and Doolin-Dalton gangs were
viewed in the same way as the James brothers. Corrupt authorities
and exploitation of law-enforcement for private ends also

characterised Lincoln County, New Mexico, but had initially Billy the Kid failed to qualify as a bandit hero. His day however was to come.

There came a point when, to those sufficiently paranoid, all America began to seem like post-Civil War Missouri writ large. By the 1920s Progressivism as a reformist movement at the national level was a spent force and its achievements in the end proved limited. The optimistic belief in limitless progress had to face involvement in the First World War. The post-war years began with race riots and a Red scare and then produced the scandals of the Harding administration. Farmers saw an irreversibly urban America, whose prosperity of the boom years up to 1929 they did not share. Prohibition, in one sense the revenge of a resentful rural America on the dominant cities, bred not merely the era of the gangster but a citizenry willing to break the law. To many Americans, filled with alarm at what the nation had become, nostalgia for the old values and a simpler age became a powerful sentiment once more. Indeed, Stephen Tatum has persuasively argued that the nostalgia for a lost age in the 1920s was stronger than in the 1890s. This new outbreak of nostalgia took several forms (religious fundamentalism was one) but inevitably part of it focussed once more on the West.

The major beneficiary was the badman and this time the West was quick to endorse the legend-making. In 1926 Frank Wilstach's *Wild Bill Hickok, Prince of the Pistoleers* was an exercise in goggle-eyed hero-worship. Some attempts at debunking the Hickok phenomenon in the same year produced an outraged response from the secretary of the Kansas State Historical Society, William E. Connelly, who six years later published his own reverent biography of Wild Bill, (deliberately omitting, as Steckmesser has demonstrated, all evidence derogatory to his hero). Hickok was established as the man who would have dealt with Al Capone with one lightning draw. Also in 1926 Robertus Love produced an admiring biography of Jesse James which combined all the known facts and all the folk tales and legends as well. Some revisions of New Mexico's incarnation of evil had begun in the twenties, but Walter Noble Burns *The Saga of Billy the Kid*, also published in 1926, effected a transformation. Now the Kid was a tragic and noble cavalier, fighting corrupt authority, driven to violence by injustice. Though it would be difficult to detect any research behind the breathless prose, Burns had interviewed survivors of the McSween faction. Now, surprise! Particularly the Mexican Americans remembered Billy with affection, though what they appear to be remembering is Charles Siringo's version of him. No matter: the Kid could now ride on, not merely as the champion of

small ranchers against wickedness in office, but also of the poor and
the minority poor at that. In 1941 *Life* magazine could begin a piece
on the Kid 'America's Best-Loved Badman.'

It was all put neatly enough by a former badman. Emmett Dalton,
surviving brother of the Dalton gang, emerged from a fourteen year
jail sentence in 1907. With the help of a ghost-writer, he produced
an autobiography in 1931. He speculated:

> Today as never before the scapegrace is the demi-hero of countless
> fictions...Why has the free-running reprobate always been so extolled?
> Is it because he symbolises the undying anarchy in the heart of almost
> every man? Because he has the rude courage of his desires? Represent
> the rogue fighting against odds – even against the police and we tacitly
> encourage him. Give him the slightest pretext of a "cause," and we
> follow in his train – in spirit at least. He becomes our fighting vicar
> against aristocracy, against power, against law, against the upstart, the
> pretender, the smugly virtuous...He becomes a very hero of democracy.

By the Depression of the 1930s, the badman of the Wild West had
come to represent, as the cowboy had in the 1890s, individualism,
self-reliance and integrity in the face of a corrupt world. His place in
the myth was permanent.

Westerners did not repudiate the myth, they exploited it. Those
clustered around the memory of Jesse James did so from the moment
of his death. His mother opened the family farmstead as a tourist
attraction and sold pebbles from his grave at five cents each. Frank
James took over this modest enterprise after her death, charged
twenty-five cents admission and sold picture postcards featuring
himself. Jesse's assassin Bob Ford went on stage to re-enact the fell
deed in a melodrama, despite threats from a shadowy group calling
itself the Avengers of Jesse James. When the play reached New York
in 1886 the *Police Gazette* reported that the theatre manager had
mounted a Gatling gun in the foyer. Ford's death in 1892 however
was the result of a saloon quarrel, not the Avengers – nor a theatre
critic. Seventy years after Billy the Kid's death, New Mexico had
commercialised a major asset and turned appropriate spots into
tourist attractions. The Kid's fenced-off grave at Fort Sumner is
complemented by an annual three-day reconstruction in Lincoln of
his escape from the town jail three months before his death.

In the 1880s and 1890s many Western towns suffered what may
be termed the Hadleyville syndrome. In the classic Western movie
High Noon, the marshal of Hadleyville fails to get the support of the
town to deal with a gang of badmen. The mayor justifies civic
inaction on the grounds that Northern investment will be discour-

aged by reports of violence in the streets. As scores of Eastern and foreign visitors' accounts reveal, in the 1880s and 1890s Western townships were desperate to shed their Wild West image. Yet, as William Savage has wryly noted, by the 1920s many of these same towns were solemnly celebrating annual frontier days, with civic dignitaries enacting, in appropriate costume, often entirely fictitious episodes of a Wild West past.

The West was not a monolith of approval for the fantasies enshrined in the myth – plenty of Westerners became increasingly critical of them. Their voices however were drowned by those who preferred a reconstructed past. When Stuart Henry, who had spent his boyhood in Abilene, criticised Emerson Hough's *North of 36* for its romanticism, he was promptly condemned by another veteran of the cattle towns for not remembering '…things as they were in that fairyland of adventure and romance'! Some believed they had a vested interest in the myth, others simply came to believe the stories they told to claim a share in it. Roosevelt once gloomily noted (his own reading tastes being suitably elevated) that every cowboy seemed to possess two pieces of literature: the *Life of Jesse James* and the current issue of the *Police Gazette*. One may speculate on how many of the old-timers whose tales found their way into print were, unconsciously or not, regurgitating items from the *Gazette*. Emmett Dalton met a judge who, not knowing his guest's identity, recounted how he had met Bob and Emmett Dalton in 1866 – five years before Emmett was born. 'He represents,' wrote Dalton, 'a type of fabricator whose "recollections" coloured much of Western lore.'

Chapter Seven

The West of the Politicians

...we tolerate no tinkering with the comfortable rationales we once worked out to justify and contain the old institutions.

Rexford Tugwell, 1934.

The difference between right and wrong seems as clear as the white hats that the cowboys in Hollywood Westerns always wore so you'd know right from the beginning who was the good guy.

Ronald Reagan, 1983

Myths show how things should be by claiming to show how they once were. If they enshrine a set of values, overtly or not they assert an ideology. They appeal in the first instance not to reason but emotion and in time they command a knee-jerk response. Taken together, these attributes guarantee that myths become woven into politics and fodder for politicians. The myth of the West was produced to serve a specific function at a specific time – to resolve the contradiction between a past in which America's values were rooted and a future where they seemed doomed to disappear. To the paranoia of the 1890s, the past was one of harmony and simplicity, the future threatened destructive conflict. Paranoia clouded judgment: America's history had been strewn with conflicts, but none of them, not even the Civil War, had wrecked the republic. Nor did the problems of the future pose insuperable difficulties to a people willing to approach them with pragmatism, flexibility and optimism. Into the problem-solving process, however, the Western myth constantly intruded.

Americans managed to make life exceptionally difficult for themselves in overcoming the problems of the twentieth century by the very device evoked to meet them. First, Americans could not decide (and still have not decided) how to reconcile their demands for government help and their resentment of government interference. Each time this dilemma has arisen, the Western myth has been trotted out to defend the sanctity of individualism and self-reliance. More importantly, the Western myth was incorporated into and made a central pillar of that structure of the imagination, the American Dream. To challenge one therefore was to imply an attack upon the other. Throughout the birth trauma of the world's most powerful industrial economy, beneath whatever was actively engaging public attention, the myth continued to resonate. No matter that some of its manifestations were now hokum and recognised by everyone as hokum – the myth survived because it was believed to be saying something crucial about America – and because the mass media continued to market it.

Whatever America thought she saw in the troubled 1890s, the nation was indeed suffering from serious weaknesses in the economy and chronic social tensions. What temporarily saved her was her belated entry into World War I. It became clear to the administration of Woodrow Wilson that, to create a war economy and supply the Allies, America would have to mobilise not just an army, but the nation. Federal government measures brought a boom to farmers and manufacturers and a potential structure for governmental regulation of the economy recognisable as necessary in any modern state. Unfortunately, a tidal wave of public opinion by 1919, fearing rising prices, labour unrest and a post-war recession, wanted a return to 'normalcy.' That was not quite what it got.

Businessmen were desperate to get rid of the wartime system of government controls and taxation and embark on a new era of expansion. They succeeded, for under three administrations after 1920, all Republican, the business community ensured first, that most of the wartime system was just dismantled and then, that it had a free hand to deal with the market and labour. One result was an economic boom, particularly in new industries, which lasted for nearly twenty years. The other was that all the old structural problems remained in industry, and with labour. Moreover, outside agribusiness, small farmers did not benefit from the new prosperity. They had raised loans to expand production for wartime exports but now found their overseas markets had disappeared in a wrecked European economy, while at the same time they were producing too much for the home market.

These trends created serious reverberations in society at large. Republican government gave businessmen a free hand but it also brought the scandals of the Harding administration. Prosperity in the cities brought the Roaring Twenties, the jazz age and contempt for hicks in the boondocks. Rural America, not sharing the prosperity, looked at the decadent cities, strikes, corruption, immigrant aliens and the collapse of the old morality with fear and rage. Its response was to revive the Ku Klux Klan (now aimed at immigrants as well as blacks), old-time religion and to impose Prohibition. This was the last gasp of nineteenth-century America in the face of the world to come. Naturally rural America clung to the Western myth, as the insatiable demand in the 1920s for rodeos, novels, and huge numbers of films testifies. The spokesman of rural America eventually became the vastly popular entertainer Will Rogers, the 'cowboy philosopher.' But business America was also willing to endorse the myth, for its values could be invoked against collectivism, labour unions and government interference. The most business-minded of presidents demonstrated this.

In 1924 President Calvin Coolidge was to head an administration whose motto he coined: 'The business of America is business.' Coolidge continued Republican aims: in his insistence on taking a lengthy daily siesta, he personified the notion that government should do as little as possible. Invariably dressed in a sober business suit, Coolidge also became noted for his extreme taciturnity, so much so that the New York wit Dorothy Parker predictably remarked on hearing of his death in 1933, 'How can they tell?' In the summer of 1927 'Silent Cal' took several weeks vacation in the Black Hills of Dakota and to mark his and the nation's birthday (he was born on 4 July) he joined a great cowboy celebration. The startling aspect of this happy event was that Coolidge appeared not only with cowboys but as one.

The *New York Times* had got wind of this unlikely event and its editorial column sarcastically remarked: 'He has already adopted a ten gallon hat. It is rumoured that he will yet appear in spurs. What if he should be so ill-advised as to don chaps, which, as every son of the West knows, are now worn only in the movies?' On 5 July at Rapid City Coolidge went the whole hog, appearing for the cameras with a horse, in a red shirt, blue bandana, silver spurs – and chaps. He and his wife were serenaded by a cowboy band which shouted at the finish 'Cal and his gal, may God be their pal.' The next day he attended a rodeo and met Indian leaders from the Pine Ridge Reservation who later made him Chief Leading Eagle of the Sioux. The *Times* was reduced to noting that though he led it everywhere, Coolidge never actually rode his horse; on 7 July he broke the tension and actually mounted the beast for a spell. The mood was soured however by an attack from the People's Business, a group founded by the late left-wing Progressive Robert M. La Follette. Its press release complained: 'The President of the United States has become a pitiful puppet of publicity. The supreme magistrate of the greatest nation on earth clownishly garbed in cowboy costume before the moving picture cameras in a vain attempt to convince the multitudes that he is a he-man!'

What explains Coolidge's extraordinary behaviour? The *Times* admitted that his reception in the West was a 'personal triumph,' but he was not seeking personal publicity, for in a startling move on 2 August he announced that he refused to run again for the Presidency in 1928. Nor was he harbouring some secret passion for the cowboy life – the *Times* remarked that the most emotion he could muster for the rodeo was 'a quizzical smile.' The likeliest explanation is that Coolidge, apart from indulging his well-known quirky sense of humour, was working on behalf of the Republicans to weaken the current widespread impression that the West was filled entirely with disaffected farmers. Indeed, on 18 July Coolidge had to endure a bitterly critical speech from the (Democrat) Governor of South Dakota on administration agricultural policies. A month later the *Times* ran an historical feature on the West which concluded that the 'new West' faced as its enemy 'not the Indian but "Wall Street", the "money interest," fat men with dollar signs embroidered on their waistcoats' and that was the West with which presidents now had to deal. Coolidge was deliberately evoking the image of Roosevelt's West, an image which transcended interests and policies and called up instant memories of admired qualities.

Many factors explain the 1928 election victory of Coolidge's successor Herbert Hoover, but it is worth noting that he carried every Western state. Hoover went on to preside over the same benign faith in business prosperity which had blinded so much of the nation since 1920. In 1929 the bubble burst and in 1931 the chickens came to home to roost. The stock market crash was a disaster, but the depression which followed was a catastrophe. The banking system collapsed, industrial production fell by half, farm incomes by two-thirds and unemployment soared – possibly to 15 million by mid-1932. The situation was catastrophic because the system seemed powerless to deal with the crisis, for not only capitalism but democracy too appeared to have failed. The worries of the 1890s were trivial by comparison: the American Dream was facing its severest test. When the Democrat Franklin Roosevelt was elected in 1932 he had no defined policy for tackling the crisis, only his promise of a 'New Deal' for the American people and insistence on the need for 'bold, persistent experimentation.' This pretty quickly translated into massive Federal government intervention in most sectors of the economy and society. Predictably, conservatives were outraged, defended the sanctity of free enterprise and prophesied the erosion of the nation's moral fibre. In the ensuing battle, both sides drew on the Western myth for ammunition. This was no time for dressing up as cowboys, for now, particularly for the political right, this was a struggle for the soul of America.

Back in 1929 the historian Frederic L. Paxson had set the tone of the argument. He insisted that America's real values '...had lasted best in what was still the West' and was optimistic that the frontier, embedded in the American character, would shape responses to the future. Those demanding change took a harder line. Robert La Follette's son Philip, in his inaugural speech as governor of Wisconsin in 1931, argued that, with the frontier gone, 'we must find our freedom and make our opportunity through wise and courageous readjustments of the political and economic order of State and Nation.' A year later Roosevelt put it specifically. Government must now control resources and distribute wealth and products because 'Our last frontier has long been reached. There is no safety-valve in the form of a western prairie...' Roosevelt's Secretary of the Interior Harold Ickes then uttered heresy: 'Rugged individualism does not mean freedom for the mass of the people, but oppression. It means the exploitation of the many by the few.'

The conservatives were horrified. They could have taken their cue from Turner himself, who back in 1914 warned that even then government intervention, though necessary, was 'endangering...the pioneer ideal of creative and competitive individualism.' James Truslow Adams wrote to the *New York Times* in March 1934 to remind America in magisterial tones of its heritage. To permit government control of economic affairs would be to sap self-reliant individualism bred in the West, pioneer qualities still vital for the present and future. Herbert Hoover took this a step further: America had not '...reached the end of the road of progress' just because the Western frontier was closed, for frontiers of the mind, in science and technology, were waiting. By 1936 Hoover was calling the New Deal a deliberate assault on 'the whole philosophy of individual liberty.'

Today this debate seems unreal. It looks perverse to argue about the heritage of the West and pioneer qualities in the midst of a crisis which struck at the roots of the nation. But it was precisely because those roots were threatened that the myth was evoked. Two contemporaries at least were however realists. In 1934 Roosevelt's adviser Rexford Tugwell exasperatedly complained that on the frontier:

virtue was made of self-dependence, of patriarchalism, of handiness in all sorts of crafts and these are still regarded as virtues in a day of collectivism, of family decay, of narrow specialization...we tolerate no tinkering with comfortable rationales we once worked out to justify and contain the old institutions.

In practical terms, as a guide to action for the crisis of the 1930s, the myth was just irrelevant. The historian Walter Prescott Webb in 1937 put his finger on why: the democracy of self-reliant individualism flourished on the frontier

> not because it solved problems, but because it seldom had to meet them...the closing of the frontier brought democratic America to the first test of its ability to govern, to solve problems rather than to enjoy an escape from them.

Whether Roosevelt's New Deal found solutions to the problems of the Depression is still debated among historians. Certainly America's entry, not quite so belated this time, into global war in 1941 gave the economy a decisive boost. This boost became a boom which eventually brought widespread prosperity that persisted until the end of the 1950s. What the New Deal had done was to give to government a huge new role, which looked to be irreversible. After the end of World War II, even the conservatives protested only how far the Federal government should intervene in the economy and society, not its right to do so: the New Deal had set the political agenda for the next thirty years.

Did all this mean that the irrelevance of the Western myth to modern America had finally been realised? Not at all. The prosperity of the 1950s produced a society broadly affluent and outwardly smugly self-satisfied. But this society knew, even if it refused to articulate it, that the price it paid for affluence was obedience to the rules of corporate business and the cost of comfortable suburbia was a stultifying conformity. Far from dying, the myth underwent a remarkable revival, as the spate of Westerns from Hollywood and on TV demonstrated. At a time when they were least visible, Americans re-affirmed the values of the frontier and, unlike the 1930s, affluence meant they could afford to parade them uncritically. Two forces were at work: the myth continued its role of allowing today's problems to be acted out in a mythical format – now on screens large and small – and the myth *became* history. Cowboys and badmen achieved their final elevation: William Savage later said of the cowboy '...approximately a century after his death as a cult object he is what is known as heritage;' and as for badmen, Wild Bill Hickok rated a reverential entry in the *Encyclopedia Americana*.

Naturally the politicians reflected all this and now drew on the myth as if it were gospel. Dwight D. Eisenhower presided over the 1950s with reluctance. He was wooed by both parties before accepting the nomination for the Republicans in 1952 and never made a secret of the fact that he disliked politics. Off-duty, what he did like was reading pulp Westerns, which he devoured at a remarkable rate. In 1953 he was disgusted and angered by a series of smear attacks on the administration and was moved to say so publicly. His speech on this occasion is often quoted but bears repeating:

> I was raised in a little town of which most of you have never heard. But in the West it is a famous place. It is called Abilene, Kansas. We had as our marshal for a long time a man named Wild Bill Hickok. If you don't know anything about him, read your Westerns more. Now that town had a code, and I was raised as a boy to prize that code. It was: meet anyone face to face with whom you disagree. You could not sneak up on him from behind, or do any damage to him, without suffering the penalty of an enraged citizenry. If you met him face-to-face and took the same risks he did, you could get away with almost anything, as long as the bullet was in front.

This spectacular example of myth in the service of politics is equally remarkable as proof of the irrelevance of historical fact. Hickok, it will be remembered, was marshal of Abilene for only a single cattle season, during which he spent most of his time gambling. Though he shot no-one in the back in 1871, his first known gunfight ten years previously made a mockery of Eisenhower's portrait. At Rock Creek Hickok carefully concealed himself and then, without warning, gunned down David McCanles and wounded his two companions, leaving only McCanles's twelve-year-old son Monroe to run away. As evidence at the time established, McCanles and his men were unarmed, a point confirmed in 1927 when Monroe McCanles, at the age of seventy-eight, wrote a dignified rebuttal to the widespread promotion of the heroic Hickok legend. To no avail – and how different Eisenhower's Abilene was from the El Paso of 1895. There, when John Sellman shot the notorious gunman John Wesley Hardin in the back, the citizenry managed to curb their outrage sufficiently (doubtless out of gratitude) to acquit Sellman of a murder charge instantly. No matter: a President of the United States would now endorse the code of the West, invented by novelists, as the rules for public life.

The complacency of the 1950s disintegrated at the decade's end. At home, the discovery of the disgrace of poverty amid plenty, civil rights activism and attacks on excessive materialism created a mood of doubt, increased by humiliations abroad. Walter Lippmann feared that America had lost any sense of a national purpose in its pursuit of pleasure; one of Eisenhower's last gestures was to set up a presidential Commission on National Goals. When John F. Kennedy won the election of 1960 (with the narrowest margin since 1888) his proclaimed intention was to bring a new vigour and direction to the United States. By this point Americans were used to presidential programmes receiving catchy titles. Back in 1903 Teddy Roosevelt had called one part of his reform programme a 'square deal' for Americans; Franklin Roosevelt found his whole domestic policy tagged the New Deal before it had begun; and his successor Harry Truman briefly called a part of his legislation the Fair Deal. Kennedy could have called his programme anything except another 'deal': he chose to call it the New Frontier.

While trying to give the impression of being the most 'modern' of leaders, Kennedy managed to call on the magnetic pull of the Western myth too. The old frontier, it was proclaimed, could have a symbolic future, because the great challenges facing the nation were analogous to the challenge of the frontier and, just like the old West, great potential lay waiting exploitation. In between radiating charisma and building Camelot, Kennedy and his paladins put together a series of initiatives to implement this vision: the Peace Corps, new economic measures to encourage growth, the Alliance for Progress, the space programme – even the Council for Physical Fitness. By committing themselves to these ventures, Americans could, they were told, once again find the old values and emerge with renewed virtue from another kind of wilderness. Where all this might have gone is impossible to judge: the inspiration for the New Frontier died, in some irony, in the modern West – with a bullet in Dallas three years later.

Kennedy's successor, Lyndon Johnson, was arguably the most Western president the United States had ever elected. Contemporaries then and biographers and historians since have commented on LBJ's constant use of metaphors and analogies from the Wild West of Texas. For five years after 1963 American politics, at home and abroad, were littered with fights with Indians, beleagured settlers and, most frequent of all, the battle of the Alamo. Johnson's biographer Doris Kearns was struck with the importance of the introduction he chose to write for his friend Walter Prescott Webb's *The Texas Rangers* in 1965. In describing the qualities of the famed Ranger Captain L.H. McNelly, Johnson defined his own sustaining belief: 'courage is a man who keeps coming on.'

What Johnson drew on was his own knowledge and memories of the Texas of the last century. So keen was he on the Alamo image that Johnson claimed in 1966 that his great-greatgrandfather had died at the siege, and when challenged corrected the location to the battle of San Jacinto – though neither was true. But Johnson had no need for inventions. His grandfather was a Texas pioneer in Blanco County, just after its formation in 1858, and ten years later was making cattle drives up to Kansas. In 1869 his grandmother hid her children while a Comanche raiding party, which had just slaughtered her neighbours, rampaged through her home; shortly afterward the men of her family wiped out the raiders at the battle of Deer Creek. Johnson himself was named after a friend of his father's who had, with great personal courage, in 1898 successfully prosecuted the notorious San Saba vigilantes. Much has been made of the impact of Johnson's background of old-time Texas violence on his conduct of U.S. foreign policy, though it is to give a great deal of weight to just one influence on a complex man and subtle politician.

One crucial fact needs stressing about all this. Unlike every president before him, Johnson was *not* evoking the myth of the West – he was calling up memories of real history, and his own family history at that. Nevertheless, the one issue which came to dominate all foreign policy in the sixties – the Vietnam War – was from start to finish permeated with fragments of the myth. Indeed, Richard Slotkin would argue that the myth governed the American response to the war. A century of seeing American progress in terms of conquering a savage land and subjugating its savage inhabitants had provided a permanent metaphor for America's destiny. That metaphor would create what Slotkin has called 'the fatal environment' of expectations and imperatives – against the forces of darkness, Americans would always win because their destiny had already been fixed. John Hellman has taken this argument a stage further: Vietnam was the last arena for Americans to enact the myth. Guilty and uneasy over their affluence and moral decay in the 1950s, Americans yearned for a return to the ideals and strength of the frontier past and thus sought new frontiers and invigorating conflict – in the Third World.

Certainly the war was permeated with the vocabulary of the myth. In 1962 Kennedy praised the men who once 'subdued a continent and wrested a civilisation from the wilderness' for now defending America 'in the jungles of Asia...' His specially-created military instruments for American involvement, the Green Berets, were written up as heroic frontiersmen with the skills of the forest hunter – and the Indian-killer. The analogies were used from the top down. Johnson reacted to the news of the Vietcong attack on Pleiku in

February 1965 with a homily from Comanche country: 'We have kept our gun over the mantel and our shells in the cupboard for a long time now. And what was the result? They are killing our men while they sleep in the night!' Army officers regularly talked to reporters of playing cowboys and Indians and one soldier, asked why he cut the ears off dead Vietcong, replied 'like scalps, you know like from Indians.' Late in the day even Henry Kissinger referred to himself as the Lone Ranger of American diplomacy and talked of extricating himself from some negotiations like a cowboy backing out of a saloon with guns drawn. John Wayne's movie *Green Berets* was in essence a Western.

Those who came to see the war not merely as a military but a moral disaster for the United States also saw it in terms of the myth. Frances Fitzgerald wrote in *Fire in the Lake* 'Americans were once again embarked on a heroic and (for themselves) almost painless conquest of an inferior race...the defeat of the Indians had seemed...the triumph of...civilization over brutish nature. Quite unconsciously, the American officers and officials used a similar language to describe the war against the NLF.' Some reversed the roles assigned by myth: Mary McCarthy saw North Vietnam as a pioneer society filled with vigour and promise and, showing some confused thinking, the war as 'a cowboys and Indians story, in which the Indians, for once, are repelling the cowboys.' The writer who most sharply linked the myth and Vietnam for the anti-war movement was however Norman Mailer. For him, Americans had lost the purifying effects of a life of nature but had stubbornly grafted frontier attitudes on to a corporate and technological society. In Mailer's bitter view, for a diseased and inwardly corrupt America, Vietnam was a logical outcome.

These broodings over a great national trauma eventually gave way to a more blatant use of the myth – by the conservatives. In 1968 Richard Nixon was elected president in part on his promise to get the United States out of Vietnam, but he also campaigned on a law-and-order platform. Nixon played on the rising fears of many Americans that Johnson's welfare programmes for blacks and poor whites, together with student protests against the war and against bureaucracy and business, were all connected to the alarming increase in urban crime. So hard did Nixon campaign on this isssue, one historian has described him as running for national sheriff. Reviewing the campaign, Theodore White wrote that Nixon reminded Americans of 'a safer past.' In his attacks on excessive government, welfare dependency and a too-liberal approach to crime, Nixon was implicitly calling on the values of the frontier and

in doing so he gave a platform to extreme right-wingers whose voices
had been muted for a decade.

Foremost among them was John Wayne. By 1970 Wayne was an
American ikon. Not only did he make more movies than any other
star – 151 excluding three Western serials back in the 1930s – but
by the time of his death in 1979 he had made eighty-nine Westerns
and had come above all to represent the popular notion of the
two-fisted cowboy, fearless in the pursuit of right and subservient
to no man. Film critics often accused Wayne of playing only himself
in his films. It looks more likely that the process was the other way
round – the more he was cast as a rugged old-fashioned conservative, the more he became one until he ended as that sad human
artifact, the man who believes his own image. This point had been
reached in May 1971 when he gave what became a notorious
interview to *Playboy*.

Wayne spelled out why the real right wing had supported Nixon.
America had gone soft, sold out by the liberals, starting with Franklin Roosevelt, who had allowed Communists to spread their evil
power abroad and to infiltrate the system at home. Their insidious
influence now reached even into the schools so that America's children were being taught to reject their heritage. Liberal weakness had
turned the Federal government into a dispenser of handouts to those
who just sat around, like blacks and Indians. 'We'll all be on a
reservation soon if the socialists keep subsidizing groups like them
with our tax money.' What was the answer? Simple, for Communism
abroad – be prepared to use nukes against the Reds in Southeast
Asia. On the home front, what was needed was a reminder of the
lessons of the frontier – history taught that Americans had only
succeeded through – of course – self-reliant individualism. Young
Americans should take as their role-models those legendary figures
who conquered the West and brushed aside impediments like Indians. 'Our so-called stealing of this country from them was just a
matter of survival...There were great numbers of people who needed
new land, and the Indians were selfishly trying to keep it for themselves.' As for the future, Americans must face the world square-on
and flinty-eyed, like the cowboys of old.

This stirring rallying cry must have interested Nixon since he had
made no secret of his admiration for Wayne and his fondness for
Wayne's Westerns. In August 1970, while attending a conference in
Denver for the Law Enforcement Assistance Administration, he
managed to link Wayne, Westerns and law-and-order. He told reporters he had just watched *Chisum*, in which Wayne played the title
role of the cattle baron in the Lincoln County war. Ignoring the film's

curious version of historical events, Nixon concentrated on the film's message: 'In the end, as this movie particularly pointed out, even in the old West…there was a time when there was no law. But the law eventually came, and the law was important from the standpoint of not only prosecuting the guilty but also seeing that those who were guilty had a proper trial.' True, Wayne's Chisum tries to work against the Santa Fé Ring using the law, but Nixon failed to stress that Chisum finally resorts to direct action (i.e. simple violence) when the law and the authorities prove corrupt – in 1970 any student radical would have used the same justification!

The Nixon-Wayne version of the West of myth clearly was in tune with a segment of public opinion. John Wayne's Westerns of the period all tended to show the same hard-bitten individualist upholding not the intricacies of the law but its staunch enforcement, and all did well at the box office. Variety's annual Top 100 list showed *True Grit* at twelfth place in 1969, *Chisum* at nineteen in 1970 and *Big Jake* at nine for 1971. Nixon understood why Westerns were a solid attraction at the box office, and indeed why Westerns had retained their immense popularity for so long. He offered no exploration of the world of myth when he concluded his chat with reporters at the Denver conference, just a single, penetrating insight: these films 'conveyed a simple but enduring moral message: the good guys come out ahead in the Westerns, the bad guys lose.' Viewpoint presumably determined reaction in August 1974, when the Watergate enquiry's escalating evidence of the administration's amazing indifference to the law finally forced Nixon's resignation. John Wayne doubtless would have seen it as another victory for the liberals, and the liberals certainly saw it as one occasion when the good guys came out ahead. Thereafter use of the Western myth in politics was muted for six years, until Ronald Reagan became the second cowboy in the White House.

Reagan's cowboy image does not really derive from his film career. He made only six Westerns, with additional appearances in television series like *Dick Powell's Zane Grey Theatre* and *Wagon Train*. At the height of his movie career, he tried hard to persuade his studio, Warners, to give him big-budget Westerns with roles like those being played by John Wayne. The studio went on giving him light comedy roles because their polls showed Reagan's appeal was mainly to women, indeed to teenage girls. When eventually he landed two major Western parts in 1953-54, he showed a flaw of which no-one ever accused John Wayne. The attribute which made him so successful as a politician was a weakness for an actor playing rugged heroes – he was too much of a nice guy. What helped to fix the cowboy image was his involvement in the television Western show, *Death Valley Days*. Taken from a radio series of the 1930s, the television version ran for twenty years from 1952 and its 532 episodes testify to its solid popularity. For two years in 1965 and 1966, Reagan acted as resident host, appropriately dressed as a cowboy. But the dress was not a costume. In his private life he acted out what he had been denied in his film career – of all choices open to him, he picked the life-style of a gentleman-rancher and was quite ready to confess that he was never so happy as when riding on his ranch. The fact was, Reagan chose to identify himself as a Westerner and as an archetype from the old West at that.

Reagan, born and raised in Illinois, moved to Hollywood in 1937. A committed New Dealer as a young man, he voted Democrat certainly up to 1950, but his involvement in politics marked his growing conservatism. By the time he was elected governor of California in 1966, he had become the spokesman for all those who were opposed to rising taxes, the growth of government and its increasing intrusions. These were the politics which took him to the White House fourteen years later and the politics and the Western image were closely bound together. The *New York Times* made a point of saying so on his inauguration in 1981. In a piece entitled 'A Cowboy Hero, Myth and Reality,' Reagan was seen as '…a politician who spent much of his time on horseback, who embraced the trappings and even the code of the frontier cowboy hero, or so it often seemed.' But the *Times* also saw clearly enough the curious mixture which made up the image:

> As Mr Reagan arrives with his posse in Washington, he is at once epitomising many of the realities of the modern West and many of the myths of the old West.

To check up on which bits of myth Reagan was epitomising, the *Times* consulted the doyen of Western historians, Ray Alan Billington. Ominously, Billington responded that they were Reagan's values, which were what he imagined were the values of the West – '…that the frontier was a land of unrestricted liberty where the individual was supreme.' This was the product of folklore but '…people believe the myth they have created and Reagan has come to personify those things.'

This was enough to give cartoonists a convenient tag for caricature. No president since Theodore Roosevelt had so regularly been typecast as a cowboy and each major moment produced the image. In 1980 a cowboy Reagan was shown as the starring 'veteran thespian' in 'Reagan Hollywood Production's' epic 'Landslide,' burying Jimmy Carter with one kick of a Texas boot; the launch of budget cuts in 1981 found him as a Western marshal holding a spare noose as a line of officials awaited hanging; over Nicaragua he frequently appeared as a sheriff or a gunfighter; the victory in Grenada produced a Reagan Hickok-style, in buckskin shirt and two huge smoking pistols; the run-up to election day in 1984 found a relaxed cowboy Reagan, twirling a pair of pistols and remarking, 'Super Tuesday, huh? Y'call *that* a showdown?'; and after the election he was shown dealing with the nation's enemies as a gunfighter from a B Western in a street shoot-out.

How much of all this had any substance? Reagan as president spoke to and for the old conservatism which had many new adherents. As the *New York Times* put it, 'He fights for individual liberty, the free enterprise system and a Federal government that will get off the backs of the people.' For the next eight years Reagan therefore continued to proclaim America's need for a revival of individualism and self-reliance and his annual messages paraded individualistic heroes. Throughout, the old West cropped up whenever a reminder was needed of its role in shaping America's destiny. Sometimes the occasion seems barely appropriate. His Mother's Day radio broadcast in 1983 reminded women that '...the Wild West could never have been tamed, the vast prairies never plowed, nor God nor learning brought to the corners of our continent, without the strength, bravery, and influence' of their forebears. He began his remarks to the National Sheriff's Association conference in 1984, 'You know, in America's frontier days the sheriff's badge was the symbol of our national quest for law and justice' – and then, since it was entirely irrelevant, sensibly never referred to the frontier again for the rest of the address.

Reagan came to the White House with more than a programme of cuts and roll-back. He offered an antidote to the disgust and sense of impotence in the face of national decline which had come to pervade America during the presidency of his predecessor, Jimmy Carter. Reagan's theme was an American renaissance – but a rebirth of what? Part of the time he implied it was of ideals and qualities, which would bring a glorious future. His second inaugural address made this clear: 'Voices are saying that we had to look to the past for the greatness and glory...[but] there is no limit to growth and human progress when men and women are free to follow their dreams.' Yet his instinct was to turn at once to the past: 'history is a ribbon, always unfurling; history is a journey. And as we continue our journey, we think of those who travelled before us...and we see and hear again the echoes of our past.' The echoes began with a brief reference to Washington and Lincoln, but turned quickly to the West:

> ...the men of the Alamo call out encouragement to each other; a settler pushes west and sings his song, and the song echoes out forever and fills the unknowing air.
>
> It is the American sound: It is hopeful, big-hearted, idealistic – daring, decent and fair. That's our heritage, that's our song. We sing it still.

Reagan did not wish to revive only the spirit of America, he wished to resurrect the past as well. In part it was the world of his youth, which in his seventies, he saw through memory's filter as secure, uncomplicated and hopeful. But that world had become enmeshed with the West of myth, which in Reagan's case was the Western. His yearning to play in Westerns went deeper than an actor's interest in meaty roles; he wrote in his autobiography:

> I thought then, and I think now, that the brief post-Civil War era when our blue-clad cavalry stayed on a war-time footing against the plains and desert Indians was a phase of Americana rivalling the Kipling era for color and romance.

The West is thus not just Warner's back lot but, in a revealing echo of Wister (the 'sagebrush Kipling') a timescape of romance.

Thirty years after Reagan had lost the chance to play Western heroes he was in a position to make the professional romanticisers national figures. Amid the distinguished group to whom Reagan awarded the Presidential Medal of Freedom in 1984, and they included the late Anwar Sadat, the former Supreme Allied Commander of Nato, Howard Baker and Eunice Kennedy Shriver, appeared the Western novelist Louis L'Amour. He was honoured because he had '...played a leading role in shaping our national identity. His writings portrayed the rugged individual and the deep-seated values of those who conquered the American frontier...[his] descriptions of America and Americans have added to our understanding of our past and reaffirmed our potential as an exploring, pioneering and free people.'

This might be thought to be the definitive expression of Reagan's beliefs about America, the West and the lessons of history. The past had best been revealed by a novelist who (the citation claimed) had sold 100 million copies of Western adventure fiction – because his brilliantly successful formula included attributes defined by myth. It would have made as much sense, if indeed not more, to make a posthumous award to John Ford – or John Wayne.

Reagan was not remarkable because he proclaimed a commitment to the imagined values of a mythic frontier – he was merely the latest president to have done so and he probably shared his beliefs with millions of his countrymen. What is remarkable is that his version of the myth is so inextricably entangled with movie images, so that the one has replaced the other. Reagan's habit of living in a mental world of old movies, and his occasional tendency to confuse real events with film scripts, is well attested. His speech at the opening of the Library of Congress exhibition on 'The Cowboy' in 1983 revealed this on a grander scale. He began with the familiar linkage of past and future, in which the West of yesterday shapes the America of tomorrow: 'If we understand this part of our history we will better understand how our people see themselves and the hopes they have for America...' Then, with the exhibits in mind, he went on:

> The difference between right and wrong seems as clear as the white hats that the cowboys in Hollywood pictures always wore, so you'd know right from the beginning who was the good guy. Integrity, morality and democratic values are the resounding themes.

For Reagan, films did not reflect history, history reflected the movies. Nearing its centennial, the myth of the West had received its most effective presidential endorsement.

Epilogue

Myth originates wherever thought and imagination are employed uncritically or deliberately used to promote social delusion.

David Bidney, 1955

The West's nostalgia for the old West still flourishes. Montana's statehood centenary in 1989 was marked by a spectacular Last Roundup, when 105 drovers pushed 2812 cattle the fifty-three miles from (where else?) Roundup to Billings, accompanied by 208 covered wagons and 2397 enthusiastic supporters. It was not quite a return to the style of a century ago: apart from the unusual human-to-cattle ratio, doctors were in attendance, helicopters available to fly out sick and injured, and caterers served meals along the trail. The event nevertheless raised $167,000 for the Montana Rural Development Fund and was viewed with great pride. Cowboy 'poetry' gatherings, for recitations of old and new cowboy verse – unkindly dismissed by critics as all 'git along, little doggerel' – have sprung up in Oklahoma City, Prescott and Flagstaff, Arizona, and Elko, Nevada. The 1989 Elko gathering, the fifth of its kind, drew 7000 participants and spectators.

Other developments seem more ominous. In the summer of 1990 the press briefly picked up an item of minor interest: the American cowboy was, it seemed, a dying breed. Wyoming cattle ranchers were bemoaning the fact that it had become impossible to hire home-grown hands. Listening to their complaints instantly suggested that, as far as the job and job-qualifications were concerned, nothing much had changed in a century. Rancher Greg Baker affirmed the old qualities: 'You've got to have someone who can be relied on. They have to be able to survive by themselves on the range when the weather turns nasty, fix fences, shoe their own horses.' Chandler Keys, Washington spokesman for the National Cattleman's Association, solemnly reminded us that 'It's rough work; not a lot of pay; long hours; a lonesome 365-day-a-year job with only a horse and a dog for company. You can't just take off for Florida for a few weeks.' Well, of course, you never could, so what had changed to produce this dearth of cowhands? The answer, it seems, was moral decay. Greg Baker was clear enough: 'We've all gotten lazy,' and even those who still saw romance on the range were now hopeless, for he added: 'A month ago we hired a young fellow from Boston but he cleared off after two weeks. Townies are always ringing up for a job, but all they want to do is ride horses off into the sunset.' Fellow-cattleman John Morris was quoted as saying, 'It is our own fault – the older generation made things too easy for them. They have become so complacent that they like everything to be mechanised, computerised, made by robots.'

This begins to sound like an unconscious repetition of one of the themes of the myth. Of course young men today expect things to be mechanised and computerised – that's progress. And progress has destroyed the old values! The press reports dug out however a more down-to-earth reason. Few cowboys earn more than $1500 per month and young Westerners can find other opportunities, without the long hours and gruelling labour, at better pay. The sacred laws of supply and demand in a free market economy suggest that cattlemen should increase wages, but it seems the profit margins on cattle-raising are now so low that this is not practicable. Frontier-bred ingenuity survives however: cattlemen are hiring skilled cowboys from Mexico and even South America, at $600-$800 per month. The Spanish Americans are happy because they are earning up to four times what they could make back home and the cattlemen are getting competent hands at half the normal wage-rates. One hundred and thirty years after it began, the Western cattle industry has returned to its roots.

If the spirit of the myth seems in the West now only to motivate ranchers, not cowboys, what is its state of health in the wider world? By the 1920s, in the definitive form it had taken a decade before, the myth seemed an indelible part of American culture. But a functional myth persists only so long as the conflict which generated it continues to fester. The Arthurian myth faded in England with the last of the Tudors and the fragmentation of unified religious belief. Spenser's *Faerie Queene* was its last great treatment, Shakespeare turned to other themes. Does the myth of the West still have relevance?

One key factor ensured the Western myth did not fade. Unlike the great functional myths of previous eras, the myth of the West coincided with the growth of modern mass media. It did not merely penetrate quickly to all parts of society and burgeon because it evoked an enthusiastic response: it proved a marketable commodity in the most market-oriented society in the world, so that its effects were re-inforced for decades by those who packaged it as a product – most notably, Hollywood. The process was mutually reinforcing. Hollywood made Westerns because Westerns made money; people watched Westerns because they found comfort in the myth; and the more Westerns that were made, the more people watched them and the more the myth was extended and reinforced. If what people sought was the image of freedom, the old values and romance in one package, then the West of the Hollywood Western was that image.

This became true for the world beyond the United States. There had been other frontiers, with wide-open spaces, bold riders, hostile natives and men with guns – in Australia, Canada, and South Africa – and some of that frontier past was romanticised. But only America had Hollywood. In 1925 the United States produced nearly 30% cent more films than the whole of the Western European countries combined, seventeen times as many as Britain, eight times as many as France and two-and-half times as many as Germany. Because Hollywood moved quickly to market its films abroad, the sheer volume of its output ensured that American films dominated Europe's cinema screens as well as those of the United States. Westerns accounted for 14% of United States film production in 1925 and were among the most popular exports. Yet when the European film industries enjoyed unprecedented expansion after World War II, American dominance was even more pronounced. By 1954 American production was only 40% of that of the Western European nations, yet the proportion of screen projection time devoted to American films had reached 65% in Italy, 70% in Britain and 85% in Ireland. In that year nearly 22% of all American films were Westerns, of which nearly all the star vehicles were exported.*

If the roots of the myth's appeal, so successfully marketed by Hollywood, lay in its capacity to evoke the values and virtues which America most feared it might lose, what accounts for its popularity outside the United States? The Marxists would claim that the universal appeal of the Western is the result of the alienation we all feel as a result of the dehumanising effects of capitalist exploitation. The conditions and patterns of work and the relationships imposed by industrial capitalism are, it is argued, unnatural and destructive of the human spirit and we instinctively long for a simpler, happier world.

---

* In the fifties, the author recalls struggling to follow the action of a Robert Ryan oater dubbed in Flemish, which turned out to be *The Proud Ones* and failing fully to appreciate Paul Newman as *Billy El Niño*.

One wonders where and when was the happy pre-industrial world Europeans yearn for. Europe's pre-industrial past was feudal and it is very hard to see the life of the masses as a rural idyll. If it was, then it is surprising that other industrial countries have not generated recent functional myths rooted in their own culture. But one looks in vain for a vast construct erected out of Merrie England or La Belle France of Henri Quatre. Europeans are outsiders looking in – at an image of a world they never had – and for them, the mythical West has been the best kind of escapism. The trappings of the myth for Americans are its essence for others – a world of open spaces, simple choices, and problems solved by direct action. The ultimate appeal of the Western film may well be, as the critic Robert Warshow long ago suggested, that it is the only genre in any medium which seriously suggests that violence solves problems. Or, as Nixon succinctly put it, 'the good guys come out ahead and the bad guys lose' – through force.

But for Americans there was more, for they never had a feudal past and they did once have a simpler world. It was not a rural idyll, but in the early nineteenth century millions of Americans did enjoy a degree of economic independence, security and opportunity unprecedented in pre-industrial societies. But not of course invariably in the late nineteenth-century West, where the myth is located and to which America's old core values were transferred. The myth has stubbornly presented the values of that world as those which made America what she is today. This is at best a dubious proposition. Industrial and, perhaps even more importantly, post-industrial societies require disciplined cooperation as well as rugged individualism, an understanding of interdependence as well as self-reliance. In the real world of international relations, statesmen and diplomats know that showdowns, confrontations at high noon and a shoot-out with the bad guys are rarely clear-cut options and standing alone is a high-risk strategy even for a superpower.

Is the Western myth thus an anachronism? Debunking the myth by showing its historical inaccuracy – a veritable industry in recent years – has not achieved much because the ultimate defence of all myth is to argue that it is true – if not literally, then in some transcendental sense. Russell Martin has written that 'it is literally true that early cowboys used guns sparingly and not very accurately, but it is *mythically* true that cowboys were adept and agile gunfighters...It is literally true that range cowboys and Indian peoples had only occasional contact with each other, but it is *mythically* true that cowboys and Indians were bitter enemies.' Martin then adds that mythic cowboys, beyond time and place, 'all of them are true, even if they never lived among us.'

Wider application of sentiments like these produces disturbing conclusions. Referring to what he calls America's 'mythic heritage,' John Hellman has noted that, because myths are extreme simplifications, they may always be easily debunked but (extending the conflict-mediatory model), asserts their function is to 'enable a nation to cohere by reconciling, in the ambiguous relations of narrative, conflicts that its people cannot solve in the sharply delineated realm of analytical thought.' From this he argues that 'Myths may often distort and conceal, but these stories are always true in the sense that they express deeply held beliefs.'

In other words, when a nation cannot resolve its inherent conflicts by rational analysis, the glue which holds it together is a set of delusions; and if enough people believe in them deeply, delusions become truth. William H. McNeill, distinguished historian and celebrated author of *Rise of the West*, put the point quite baldly. Myth, he wrote, '...is mankind's substitute for instinct' and

A people without a quiver of relevant agreed-upon statements, accepted through education or less formalized acculturation, soon finds itself in deep trouble, for, in the absence of believable myths, coherent public action becomes very difficult to improvise or sustain.

This line of argument is hauntingly familiar. It is Plato's famous suggestion that a stable state needs a state religion, suitably manufactured if necessary, to ensure social unity. His phrase for this used to be translated as the 'noble lie.' It is an unflattering comment on a democratic people's ability to order its society and government to argue that it can be managed only by general subscription to a set of inventions. Forty years ago the authority on myth, David Bidney, wrote:

Myth must be taken seriously as a cultural force but it must be taken seriously precisely in order that it may be gradually superseded in the interests of the advancement of truth and the growth of human intelligence.

Myth cannot indefinitely act as a substitute for a sense of history. Americans have long abandoned their early belief that history was irrelevant for them and have recognised that no nation can cut itself off from its past – for the very practical reason that every people needs a sense of the forces which have shaped the present and in some measure must determine aspects of the future. But what happens, as Gary Wills has asked, 'if, when we look into our historical rearview mirror, all we can see is a movie?'

BIBLIOGRAPHY

Abbott, E.C. and Helena H. Smith, *We Pointed Them North: Recollections of a Cowpuncher* (New York, 1939)

Abbott, John S.C., *Christopher Carson, Familiarly Known as Kit Carson* (New York, 1873)

Adams, Andy, *The Log of a Cowboy* (Boston & New York, 1903)

Adams, Ramon and Homer Britzman, *Charles M. Russell, the Cowboy Artist: a Biography* (Pasadena, Cal., 1948)

Allen, Douglas and D. Allen, Jnr., *N.C. Wyeth* (New York, 1972)

'Alter, Judith, 'Rufus Zogbaum and the frontier West' *Montana: the Magazine of Western History* 1973 vol. 23, no. 4., pp. 42-53

Anderson, Harry H., 'Deadwood, South Dakota: an effort at stability', *Montana: The Magazine of Western History* 1970 vol. 20, Jan., pp. 40-47

Asbaugh, Don, *Nevada's Turbulent Yesterday* (Los Angeles, 1963)

Athearn, Robert G., *The Mythic West in Twentieth-Century America* (Lawrence, Kan., 1986)

Aveling, Edward and Eleanor Marx Aveling, *The Working Class Movement in America* (London, 1888)

Bank, Rosemarie M., 'Melodrama as a social document: social factors in the American frontier play' *Theater Studies* 1975-76 vol. 22 pp: 42–49

Bartlett, Richard A., *The New Country: A Social History of the American Frontier 1776-1890* (New York, 1976)

Bataille, Gretchen M. and Charles L.P. Silet, (eds.) *The Pretend Indians: Images of Native Americans in the Movies* (Ames, Iowa, 1980)

Baumann, John, 'On a Western Ranche' *Fortnightly Review* 1887, vol. 46 pp. 516-533

        'Experiences of a cow-boy' *Lippincott's Magazine* Sept. 1886

Billington, Ray Allan, *America's Frontier Heritage* (New York, 1966)

        Frederick Jackson Turner: Historian, Scholar, Teacher (New York, 1973)

        Land of Savagery, Land of Promise (New York, 1981)

Bird, Isabella L., *A Lady's Life in the Rocky Mountains* (Norman, Okla., 1960)

Bluestone, G., 'The changing cowboy: from dime novel to dollar film' *Western Humanities Review* 1960 vol. 14, Summer, pp. 331-337

Boatwright, Mody C., 'The formula in cowboy fiction and drama' *Western Folklore* 1969 vol. 28, no.2, pp. 136-145

'The Western badman as hero' *Publications of the Texas Folklore Society* 1975 vol. 27, pp. 96-165

Boatright, Mody, W.M. Hudson and A. Maxwell, (eds.), *Mesquite and Willow* (Dallas, 1957)

Bragin, Charles, *Dime Novels, 1860-1964* (New York, 1964)

Branch, Douglas, *The Cowboy and his Interpreters* (New York, 1961)

Briggs, John E., 'Pioneer Gangsters' *Palimpsest* 1940 vol. 21, pp. 73-99

Brown, Richard Maxwell, *Strain of Violence: Historical Studies of American Violence and Vigilantism* (New York, 1975)

Brownlow, Kevin, *The War, the West and the Wilderness* (London, 1979)

Burnside, Wesley, *Maynard Dixon, Artist of the West* (Provo, Ut., 1974)

Calder, Jenni, *There Must Be a Lone Ranger* (London, 1974)

Cawelti, John G., 'The gunfighter and society' *American West* 1968 vol. 5, March, pp. 30-35, 76-78

The Six-gun Mystique (Bowling Green, Ohio, 1971)

Clark, Barrett H., *America's Lost Plays*, 21 vols., (Bloomington, Ind. 1963-65, 1969)

Cody, William Frederick, *The Life of the Hon. William Frederick Cody Known as Buffalo Bill, the Famous Scout and Guide: an Autobiography* (Hartford, Ct., 1879)

Cohen, Hennig (ed.), *The American Experience* (Boston, 1968)

Cronon, William, G. Miles and J. Gitlin, *Under an Open Sky: Rethinking America's Western Past* (New York, 1992)

Currie, Barton W., 'Bandits lone and otherwise' *Harper's Weekly* 12 Sept. 1908

Dale, Edward E. *The Range Cattle Industry* (Norman, Okla., 1960)

Dalton, Emmett and J. Jungmeyer, *When the Daltons Rode* (New York, 1931)

Davis, Richard H., *The West from a Car Window* (New York, 1892)

Davy, David, *Cowboy Culture: A Saga of Five Centuries* (New York, 1981)

Deutsch, J.I., 'Jesse James in dime novels: ambivalence towards an outlaw hero' *Dime Novel Roundup* 1976 vol. 45, Feb., pp. 2-11

Dodge, Richard I., *Our Wild Indian: Thirty-three Years Personal Experience among the Redmen of the Great West* (Hartford, Ct., 1882)

Dorson, R.M., 'Davy Crockett in the Heroic Age' *Southern Folklore Quarterly* 1942, vol. 6, pp. 95-102

Drago, Henry Sinclair, *The Great Range Wars: Violence on the Grasslands* (New York, 1970)

Drinnon, Richard, *Facing West: The Metaphysics of Indian Hating and Empire Building: A Major Investigation of the Historical Link Between American Racism and Expansionism* (Minneapolis, 1980)

Durham, Philip, 'The Cowboy and the Myth-Makers' *Journal of Popular Culture* 1967 vol. 1, pt.1, pp. 58-72

'Dime novels: an American heritage' *Western Humanities Review* 1954-55 vol. 9 pp. 33-43

Dykes, J.C., 'Dime Novel Texas: or The Sub-Literature of the Lone Star State' *Southwestern Historical Quarterly* 1946 vol. 46, no.3, pp. 327-340

Dykstra, Robert R., *The Cattle Towns: a Social History of the Cattle Trading Centers* (New York, 1968)

Egan, Ferol Raymond, 'The place of the cowboy novel in American literature: a study of its developmental form, 1900 to 1950' [unpublished thesis, College of the Pacific]

Eliade, Mircea, *Myth and Reality* (London, 1964)

Elkin, Frederick, 'The psychological appeal of the Hollywood Western' *Journal of Educational Sociology* 1950 vol. 24, no.2, pp. 72-86

Elliott, Mabel A., 'Crime and the frontier mores' *American Sociological Review* 1944 vol. 9, April, pp. 185-192

Elman, Robert, *Bad Men of the West* (New York, 1974)

Etulain, Richard, 'The Development of the Western' *Journal of Popular Culture* 1973 vol. 7, no.3, pp 647-651, 717-726

'Origin of the Western' *Journal of Popular Culture* 1972 vol. 5, no.4, pp. 797-805

The Popular Western: Essays Towards a Definition (Bowling Green, Ohio 1974)

Evans, John W., 'Modern man and the cowboy' *Television Quarterly* 1962 vol. 1, May, pp. 31-41

Falk, Odel B., *Tombstone: Myth and Reality* (London, 1972)

Fenin, George N. and William K. Everson, *The Western: from Silents to Cinerama* (New York, 1972)

Fishwick, Marshall, *The Hero, American Style* (New York, 1969)

Folsom, James K., *The Western: a Collection of Critical Essays* (Englewood Cliffs, N.J., 1979)

Frantz, Joe B. and J.E. Choate, *The American Cowboy: the Myth and the Reality* (Norman, Oklahoma, 1955)

French, Warren, 'The cowboy in the dime novel' *University of Texas Studies in English* 1951 vol. 30 pp. 219-234

Gerster, Patrick and Nicholas Cords, *Myth in American History* (Encino, Cal., 1977)

Goetzmann, W.H., 'The mountain man as Jacksonian man' *American Quarterly* 1963 vol. 15 pp. 402-415

Goetzmann, W.H. and W.N. Goetzmann *The West of the Imagination* (New York and London, 1986)

Graham, H.D. and T.R. Gurr (eds.), *The History of Violence in America* (New York, 1969)

Grohman, W. Bailie, 'Cattle Ranches in the Far West' *Fortnightly Review* 1880 vol. 34 pp. 447-457

Hagedorn, Hermann, *Roosevelt in the Badlands* (Boston, 1921)

Hamilton, Clayton, 'Melodrama, old and new' *Bookman* 1911 vol. 33, May, pp. 309-314

Hardy, Phil, *The Western* (London, rev. ed. 1991)

Harris, C.W. and W.G. Rainey, *The Cowboy: Sixshooters, Songs and Sex* (Norman, Oklahoma, 1976)

Harger, Charles M., 'Cattle-Trails of the Prairies' *Scribner's Magazine* 1892 vol. 11, June, pp. 732-742

Harvey, C.M., 'The dime novel in American life' *Atlantic Monthly* 1907 vol.100, July, pp. 37-45

Hassrick, Peter H., *Frederic Remington* (New York, 1973)

Hawgood, John, *The American West* (London, 1967)

Hellman, John, *The American Myth and the Legacy of Vietnam* (New York, 1986)

Hine, Robert V., *The American West: an Interpretive History* (Boston, 1973)

Holden, William C., 'Law and lawlessness on the Texan frontier, 1875-1890' *Southwestern Historical Quarterly* 1940 vol. 44, Oct., pp. 188-203

Hollon, W. Eugene, *Frontier Violence: Another Look* (New York, 1974)

Horan, James D., *The Authentic Wild West: the Gunfighters* (New York, 1976)

The Authentic Wild West: the Outlaws (New York, 1977)

Hough, Emerson, *The Passing of the Frontier* (New Haven, Ct., 1918)

The Story of the Outlaw (New York, 1918)

Hughes, Glenn, *A History of the American Theatre* (New York, 1951)

Hunter, J. Marvin, (ed.), *The Trail Drivers of Texas* 2 vols., (San Antonio, Tex., 1920-23)

Hyams, Jay, *The Life and Times of the Western Movie* (Columbus, Okla., 1983)

Hyde, Albert E., 'The old regime in the Southwest: the reign of the revolver' *Century* 1912 vol. 43 pp. 690-701.

Jacobson, Larry K., 'The mythic origins of the Western' [unpublished doctoral dissertation, U. of Minnesota 1973)

James, Will S., *Cow-Boy Life in Texas, or 27 Years a Mavrick* (Chicago, 1893)
Jameson, Frederic, 'Ideology, narrative analysis and popular culture' *Theory and Society* 1977, Winter, pp. 543-559
Johannsen, Albert, *The House of Beadle and Adams and its Dime and Nickle Novels: the Story of a Vanished Literature*, 3 vols. (Norman, Okla., 1950-1962)
Jones, Daryl, 'Blood 'n thunder: virgins, villains and violence in the dime novel western' *Journal of Popular Culture* 1970 vol. 4, Fall, pp. 507-517
           'Clenched teeth and muttered curses: revenge and the dime novel outlaw hero' *Journal of Popular Culture* 1975 vol. 7. Winter, pp. 652-665
           The Dime Novel Western (Bowling Green, Ohio, 1978)
Jussim, Estelle, *Frederic Remington, the Camera and the Old West* (Fort Worth, Tex., 1983)

Katz, William L., *The Black West* (Garden City, N.Y., 1971)
Keleher, W.A., *The Fabulous Frontier* (Santa Fe, N.M., 1945)
           Violence in Lincoln County, 1869-1881 (Albuquerque, N.M., 1957)
Kirkpatrick, J.M., *Timothy Flint: Pioneer, Missionary, Author, Editor, 1780-1840* (Cleveland, O., 1911)
Klapp, Orin 'The clever hero' *Journal of American Folklore* 1954 vol. 67, June, pp. 21-34
Kruse, H.H., 'Myth in the making: the James brothers, the bank robbery at Northfield and the dime novel' *Journal of Popular Culture* 1978 vol. 8, Fall, pp. 315-325

Lacey, Norris J. and G. Ashe, *The Arthurian Handbook* (New York and London, 1988)
Lambert, Neal, 'The values of the frontier: Owen Wister's final assessment' *South Dakota Review* 1971 vol. 1, Spring, pp. 76-87
Lawrence, J., 'Jesse James v. East Lynne' *Billboard* 1919 vol. 22, March, pp. 33, 208, 209
Leach, Joseph, 'The paper-back Texan, father of the American Western hero' *Western Humanities Review* 1957 vol. 11, Summer, pp. 267-275
Leithead, E., 'The outlaws rode hard in dime novel days' *American Book Collector* 1968 vol. 19, December, pp. 13-19
Lévi-Strauss, Claude, *Structural Anthropology* (N.Y., 1967)
Lewis, Alfred H., *Wolfville Nights* (New York, 1902)
Limerick, Patricia N., *The Legacy of Conquest: the Unbroken Past of the American West* (New York, 1987)
Love, Nat, *The Life and Adventures of Nat Love* (rep. New York, 1968)

Martin, Russell, *Cowboy: the Enduring Myth of the Wild West* (New York, 1983)

Mattison, R.M., 'Roosevelt and the Stockmen's Association' *North Dakota History* 1950 vol. 17 pp. 81-85

McCauley, James Emmett, *A Stove-up Cowboy's Story* (Austin & Dallas, Texas, 1943)

McCoy, Joseph G., *Historic Sketches of the Cattle Trade of the West and Southwest* (Kansas City, Mo., 1874)

McDermott, J.F. (ed.), *The Frontier Re-examined* (Urbana. Ill., 1967)

McGrath, Roger, *Gunfighters, Highwaymen and Vigilantes* (Berkeley, Cal., 1984)

McNeill, William H., 'The care and repair of public myth' *Foreign Affairs* 1982 vol.61, Fall, pp. 1-13

Milton, John, *The Novel of the American West* (Lincoln, Neb., 1980)

Merriman, J.D., *The Flower of Kings: a Study of the Arthurian Legend in England between 1485 and 1835* (Lawrence, Kan. 1973)

Metz, Leon C., *Pat Garrett: the History of a Western Lawman* (Norman, Okla., 1974)

Meyer, R.E., 'The outlaw: a distinctive American folktype' *Journal of the Folklore Institute* 1980 vol. 17, MayDec., pp. 94-124

Miller, Nyle H., E. Langsdorf and R.W. Richmond (eds.), *Kansas in Newspapers* (Topeka, Kan., 1963)

Miller, Nyle H. and J.W. Snell, *Why the West was Wild: a contemporary look at the antics of some highly publicised Kansas cowtown personalities* (Topeka, Kan., 1963)

Monaghan, Jay, *The Great Rascal: the Life and Adventures of Ned Buntline* (New York, 1951)

Mondy, R.W., 'Analysis of frontier instability' *Southwestern Social Science Quarterly* 1942 vol. 24, Sept., 167-177

Mordden, Ethan, *The American Theatre* (New York, 1981)

Morris, Edmund, *The Rise of Theodore Roosevelt* (London, 1979)

Mott, Frank L., *The History of American Magazines* (Cambridge, Mass., 1930)

Mottram, Eric, '"The Persuasive Lips": men, guns in America, the West' *Journal of American Studies* 1976 vol. 10, pt. 1, pp. 53-84

Mullen, R.N. and Charles E. Welch, 'Billy the Kid: the making of a hero' *Western Folklore* 1973 vol. 32, pp. 104-112

Munden, Kenneth, J., 'A contribution to the psychological understanding of the origin of the cowboy and his myth' *American Imago* 1958 vol. 15 pp. 103-148

Nachbar, Jack (ed.), *Focus on the Western* (Englewood Cliffs, N.J., 1974)

Nash, Roderick, *Wilderness and the American Mind* (New Haven Ct. 1982)
Nimmo, Joseph Jr., 'The American Cowboy' *Harper's New Monthly Magazine* 1886 vol. 57, Nov., pp. 880-884
R.W. Norton Art Gallery, *Frederic Remington: Paintings, Drawings and Sculpture* (Shreveport, La., 1979)
Nussbaum, Martin, 'The sociological symbolism of the "adult" western' *Social Forces* 1960 vol. 39, pt. 1, pp. 25-28
Nye, Russell, *The Unembarrassed Muse: the Popular Arts in America* (New York, 1970)

Opie, John, *The Law of the Land: Two Hundred Years of American Farmland Policy* (Lincoln, Neb., 1987)

Pender, Lady Rose, *A Lady's Experiences in the Wild West in 1883* (London, 1888)
Prassell, Frank, *The Western Peace Officer* (Norman, Okla., 1972)
Puttnam, Carleton, *Theodore Roosevelt: the Formative Years, 1858-1886* (New York, 1958)

Reddin, Paul L., 'Wild West shows: a study in the development of Western romanticism' [unpublished doctoral thesis, Unversity of Missouri, 1970}
Renner, Frederick S., *Charles M. Russell* (New York, 1974)
Reisner, Mark, *Cadillac Desert: the American West and its Disappearing Water* (New York, 1986)
Richthofen, Walter, baron von, *Cattle-raising on the Plains of North America* (new ed., Norman, Okla., 1964)
Ross, T.J., 'Fantasy and form in the Western: from Hart to Peckinpah' *December* 1970 vol.12, Fall, pp. 158-169
Robinson, F.G., 'The Roosevelt-Wister connection' *Western American Literature* 1979 vol. 14 pp. 95-114
Rollins, Philip A.*The Cowboy: an Unconventional History of Civilisation on the Old-Time Cattle Range* (New York, 1922)
Roosevelt, Theodore *Ranch Life and the Hunting Trail* (New York, 1888)
Rosa, Joseph G., *They Called Him Wild Bill: the Life and Adventures of James Butler Hickok* (Norman, Okla., 1978)
Roberts, Gary L., 'The West's gunmen' *American West* 1971, vol. 8, Jan. and March, 10-15, 64; 18-23, 61-62
Russell, Austin, *Charles, Russell, Cowboy Artist* (New York, 1957)
Russell, Don, *The Lives and Legends of Buffalo Bill* (Norman, Okla., 1960)
   The Wild West: a History of the Wild West Shows (Fort Worth, Tex., 1970)

Samuel, Peggy and Harold Samuel, *Frederic Remington: a Biography* (Garden City, N.Y., 1982)
Sarf, Wayne M., *God Bless You Buffalo Bill* (East Brunswick, N.J., 1983)

Savage, W.W., Jr., *Cowboy Life: Reconstructing an American Myth* (Norman, Okla., 1975)
> *The Cowboy Hero: His Image in American History and Culture* (Norman, Okla., 1979)

Schein, Harry, 'The olympian cowboy' *American Scholar* 1955 vol. 24, pt.3, pp. 309-320

Schwartz, Joseph, 'The Wild West show: "everything genuine"' *Journal of Popular Culture* 1970 vol. 3, pt.4, pp. 656-666

Sebeok, Thomas (ed.), *Myth: a Symposium* (Bloomington, Ind., 1955)

Shapiro, M.E. and P.H. Hassrick, *Frederic Remington: the Masterworks* (Network, 1988)

Siringo, Charles, *A Texas Cowboy, or, Fifteen Years on the Hurricane Deck of a Spanish Pony* (Chicago, 1885))

Slotkin, Richard, *Regeneration through Violence: the Mythology of the American Frontier, 1600-1860* (Middletown, Ct., 1973)
> *The Fatal Environment: the Myth of the Frontier in the Age of Industrialisation* (New York, 1985)
> *Gunfighter Nation: the Myth of the Frontier in Twentieth Century America* (New York, 1992)

Smith, Gene and Joyce Barry *The Police Gazette* (New York, 1972)

Smith, Harry J., 'The melodrama' *Atlantic Monthly* 1907 vol. 99, March, pp. 320-328

Smith, Henry Nash, *The Virgin Land: the American West in Symbol and Myth* (Cambridge, Mass., 1950)

Sonnichsen, C.L., *From Hopalong to Hud: Thoughts on Western Fiction* (College Station, Tex., 1978)

Steckmesser, Kent, 'Robin Hood and the American outlaw' *Journal of American Folklore* 1966 vol. 79, April-June, pp. 348-355
> *The Western Hero in History and Legend* (Norman, Okla., 1965)
> *Western Outlaws: the "Good Badman" in Fact, Fiction and Folklore* (Claremont, Ca., 1983)

Stiffer, Stuart A., 'Davy Crockett: the genesis of a heroic myth' *Tennessee Historical Quarterly* 1957 vol. 16 pp. 134-140

Taft, Robert, *Photography and the American Scene* (New York, 1964)

Tait, James, *The Cattlefields of the Far West: their Present and Future* (Edinburgh and London, 1884)

Tatum, Stephen, *Inventing Billy the Kid: Visions of the Outlaw in America* (Albuquerque, N.M., 1982)

Taylor, Lonn and Ingrid Marr, *The American Cowboy* (Washington, D.C., 1983)

Thorp, Raymond M., 'Hero-maker of the Old West' *Old West* 1965 vol. 1, no. 4, pp. 16-17, 56-57

Topping, Gary, 'Zane Grey: a literary assessment' *Western American Literature* 1978 vol. 13 pp. 51-64

    'Zane Grey's West' *Journal of Popular Culture* 1973 vol. 7, pt.3, pp. 681-689

Van Dyke, John C., *The Open Spaces* (New York, 1922)

Vorpahl, Ben M., *Frederic Remington and the West* (Austin, Tex., 1978)

    "My Dear Wister": The Frederic Remington-Owen Wister Letters (Palo Alto, Cal., 1972)

Waldmeier, J.J., 'The cowboy, the knight and popular taste' *Southern Folklore Quarterly* 1958 vol. 22, pt. 3, pp. 113-120

Walker, Don D., *Clio's Cowboys: Studies in the Historiography of the Cattle Trade* (Lincoln, Neb., 1981)

    'Riders and reality: a philosophical problem in the autobiography of the cattle trade' *Western Historical Quarterly* 1978 vol. 9 pp. 163-179

Warshow, Robert, *The Immediate Experience: Movies, Comics, Theatre and Other Aspects of Popular Culture* (Garden City, N.Y., 1962)

Webb, Walter *The Great Plains* (New York, 1931)

Wecter, Dixon, *The Hero in America: a Chronicle of HeroWorship* (Ann Arbor, Mich., 1966)

West, Elliott, 'Good guys, bad guys: the movie Western and the popular mind' *Film and History* 1975 vol. 5 pp. 1-5, 13

Westermeier, C.P. *Trailing the Cowboy: His Life and Lore as Told by Frontier Journalists* (Caldwell, Id., 1935)

Weston, Jack *The Real American Cowboy* (New York, 1985)

White, G. Edward, *The Eastern Establishment and the Western Experience: the West of Frederic Remington, Theodore Roosevelt and Owen Wister* (New Haven, Ct., 1968)

White, R., 'Outlaw gangs of the middle border' *Western Historical Quarterly* 1981 vol. 12 pp. 387-408

Wister, Fanny Kemble, *Owen Wister Out West: His Journals and Letters* (Chicago, 1958)

Wister, Owen, 'The evolution of the cowboy, *Harper's Monthly Magazine* 1895, Sept., pp. 606, 608

    The Virginian: a Horseman of the Plains (New York, 1902)

Woods, Lawrence M. *British Gentlemen in the Wild West: the Era of the Intensely English Cowboy* (London, 1990)

Wright, Will, *Six Guns and Society: a Structural Study of the Western* (Berkeley and Los Angeles, 1975)

Index